New Mum's
Guide to
Sex

The
New Mum's
Guide to
Sex

Rediscover Passion
After Childbirth

Rachel Foux

First published in 2007 by Fusion Press,
a division of Satin Publications Ltd
101 Southwark Street
London SE1 0JF
UK
info@visionpaperbacks.co.uk
www.visionpaperbacks.co.uk
Publisher: Sheena Dewan

A catalogue record for this book is available
from the British Library.

ISBN: 978-1-905745-13-5

2 4 6 8 10 9 7 5 3 1

Cover and text design by ok?design
Cover illustrations by Kate Pollard
Printed and bound in the UK by
Mackays of Chatham Ltd, Chatham, Kent

To my beautiful children, Sebastian and Eloise

Contents

Acknowledgements

I want to thank everyone who spoke up when I asked them to tell me the truth about sex after babies. You were very brave and honest and I couldn't have written this book without your invaluable help. I have such gratitude to my husband, Trevor, for your rock-solid love and support; to Tinu, for your dogged encouragement; to Harriet, for getting me started; to Rob, for inspiring me; and to Lisa, Pete and Cathy for your generosity of spirit. I also want to acknowledge and thank my teachers in the Deer Tribe Metis Medicine Society as well as Yehudi Gordon and Dr Gowri Motha for her innate wisdom about pregnant women. Thank you also to the great team at Vision for helping my words become accessible and to Liz Puttick, my agent, for remembering me. Last but not least, my children, Ella and Seb – without you guys in my life, I would never have understood how to be a sexy mummy.

Introduction

When I think back to having my own babies, I wish that I could have had a book like this, as nobody told me anything about sex after childbirth — at least, not in the detail that I would have liked. I didn't just want to know when I was allowed to have sex again, I was looking for a way to integrate my new role as a mum into my sex life and vice versa and I definitely didn't find this in any pregnancy or baby book. Lucky for me, through a bit of trial and error I worked out a way to cope in those dark years of early motherhood by prioritising my own needs, which led me to become a sexy and confident mum.

As I see it, sexuality isn't just about the act of making love; it touches everything that we do. It is our greatest gift and lights up us and all those around us. Sex is the creative life force that burns in our bellies, before, during and after we give birth. But if we are not awake enough in ourselves to recognise our passion, it could burn out and that would be a shame for humanity and our families — being brought up by parents who no longer love each other is no fun for your children.

I feel privileged to have had such fantastic clients for more than a decade, who have shared one of the most intimate times in their lives with me, namely their child birthing years. I've observed some families grow from being a couple to being a family of four, five and six and all the adventures that these changes have brought along the way. I have been privy to some of their most personal stories and I thank you all from the bottom of my heart for sharing your secrets with me.

I know from personal experience just how much stress having a baby can bring to an intimate relationship. I realised early on in my career as a mother that if I was going to get through the early years with my relationship still intact, some serious strategies for survival would have to be implemented. This may give you the impression that I was preparing for war and to be honest, there were times when it felt like I was. But it was determination and discipline that pulled my relationship with my partner to a brighter and better place, despite our near exhaustion. I wish the same for you, without the exhaustion and I'm very happy to be able to offer you this helping hand along the way.

Introduction

It's tempting to want to just sit back and wait for these times to pass, but this wouldn't be a successful formula. I know this to be true as it's these parents who put their relationship and intimacy under the carpet after their children were born that I've met as a sex therapist. It's not my intention to frighten you with this, but you need to know how hard these brave couples had to work to get their sexual connection back after years of ignoring it. I believe that it really doesn't have to be this way. If you can put your attention on your own sexual needs and desires from the beginning of your journey as parents, then the rest will follow. It's when we forget that we are first and foremost sexual beings, as well as parents, that the trouble can hit.

From the very first chapter, I will invite you to take responsibility for yourself as a sexual woman and mother. It's the best way to break down our belief systems about how mums should or shouldn't behave. In particular, the pattern many of us have of letting our personal needs be less important than the needs of our family. Month by month, I will encourage you to look for opportunities to give yourself treats that will help you to heal and strengthen from the birth and to find your place as a woman of power, rather than a downtrodden mum. I want you to aim for your highest potential, so that you can be in the best possible shape to be an excellent mum and partner. Have you noticed that whenever you are feeling really good about yourself, that you become much more attractive out in the world and in your relationship?

I don't want to push you to make big, scary leaps in your relationship during this time – it's already scary enough. Rather, take little steps each month to get to know each other again as lovers, not just parents. I'm quite realistic about what you can achieve, particularly in the early days, but what counts is how often you actually manage to spend quality time together. I will remind you to prioritise this and then encourage you both to spend this time, either communicating your emotions or building up your repertoire of sensual, intimate knowledge about each other.

To help you to get the most from this book everyday, come rain or shine, I have included lots of tips and suggestions for you and your partner. These stand out from the main text, but they also help to highlight important points in my discourse. Hopefully, you'll to be able to dip in and out at your leisure but still get something of substance to chew over as you go about your daily life as a mum.

It may appear at first glance that this book is written exclusively for mums, especially with a title like *The New Mum's Guide to Sex*. But this isn't the case – far from it. I want all dads to know that they are very welcome to read the book too, so I have highlighted tips that may be specifically helpful for him.

You'll notice that the book is also broken up into 'Lovers tip', 'Couple tip' and 'Couple time'. The 'Lovers tip' is just that — a nugget of advice about sex to you as lovers, not as Mum and Dad. 'Couple tip' sections address issues that most couples are likely to be confronting in these post-natal months and for this reason, I would suggest that you read them out loud together. Lastly, 'Couple time' boxes are the most fun parts of the book, as they get you to do little exercises together as a couple.

Every exercise and tip in this book has the potential to keep the flame of passion burning between you, albeit on a low light. It's too easy to let this flame go out and to find yourselves living together like brother and sister. I am ever optimistic that even the lowest burning flame is easier to reignite than a fire that has gone out completely. I encourage you to see this too and to read on.

1

Late Pregnancy

You may be at the beginning of this book but it's unlikely that you'll be at the beginning of your pregnancy. The best time to start reading would be after you've had your fill of every 'How-to' baby and birth book on the planet. This chapter isn't about telling you how you can have a great sex life. You will need to work this out for yourselves. I know that you know how, it's simply a matter of remembering what to do. Unfortunately there is very little help and support for relationships, especially sexually intimate ones, in our society. So you have no choice but to become the pioneers of change and take responsibility for your own destiny during these nine months.

From day one of the pregnancy we're continually bombarded with the how and why of what we should be feeling. Yet our own internal dialogue alone does enough talking to last the full nine months. Let's face it, falling pregnant, regardless of how hard you did or didn't try, is a complete shock to the system. It really doesn't matter if this is your first or fifth child, the shock will still be there. It sprawls out into your relationship with your partner, your work life and into your friendships and family connections.

But not all shocks are bad things. They help to catalyse us into making powerful changes in our lives. Nobody can argue that becoming parents together doesn't do this. So why is it that we seem to hear only stories about what a disaster our relationship and sex life will be when we're parents? Where are the stories of power and success? And why do we choose to buy into this mindset and forget to take advantage of what we have and know – the actual power of our intimate bond?

When we came together with our partners, we celebrated our togetherness. Whether there was an official ceremony or not, it became obvious that our lives had changed. We were two rather than one. It's because of this togetherness that we become three, four and five. And although this may seem simplistic, somewhere between the pregnancy test stick and the labour room, we can forget about our powerful connection together. From time to time, you will have had glimpses of it through the pregnancy, like when you told the world your ecstatic news, or shared those first glimpses of your child on the ultrasound or heard the first heartbeat.

Afterwards, it seems that we retreat back to our personal whirlwinds.

Imagine if we were able to download the full spectrum of thoughts that pass through the minds of prospective parents over the nine months of pregnancy and enabled them to mingle with each other in cyberspace. It could potentially be quite explosive up there.

♀♂ **Couple time**

Just for fun, take your pen and draw a picture of the two of you, something like the one overleaf. Grab a pen and some paper and take it in turns to scribble down all the emotions that are running around in your heads today, especially the ones that involve the pregnancy. Then imagine how it would feel to stand in the space between you both, surrounded by these feelings. Your relationship lives in this space. Yes, it also lives in your hearts and minds but it's here where the action really happens. It will have changed from before you became pregnant – more cramped for a start and this can be physically uncomfortable for a time. Did you notice how some of the discomfort has melted away now that you talked about it together?

Here are a few examples from your fellow prospective parents:

Woman

- Who will I be?
- Will I cope with birth and being a mum?
- I'm scared. I'm confused.
- I hate sex.
- I'm so horny. Does he still fancy me?
- I feel fat and ugly.
- I've never felt so sexy and confident.

Man

- Will I be able to protect them?
- I'm already lonely.
- I wonder what it will be like.
- Sex is a turn-off.
- I'm bored by the constant talk about babies.
- I'm stressed about providing.
- I'm afraid I'll hurt the baby if we have sex.

BODY IMAGE DURING PREGNANCY

Pregnancy changes a lot for us but unfortunately the desire to be super slim and sexy doesn't seem to change for most women. This is pretty unfortunate as an increase in size is an inevitable part of being pregnant, as you'll now know. There are plenty of glossy pregnancy magazines packed with images of beautiful, round and sexy women. Yes, they have clear skin, sparkling eyes and no bags under their eyes but they are still pregnant and proud of it, or so we are led to believe. The sad thing is that the majority of women become dissatisfied with their appearance during pregnancy, whether they've put on lots of weight or not. The change in body shape, the expanding waistline and sagging breasts can be too upsetting for words. But who can you talk to about these feelings? Try your partner. You might be surprised at their response.

If we can embrace the way we look and accept ourselves, bumps and all, it is a more relaxing way to live. If we're happy about the way you look, we'll feel much sexier. In fact we'll radiate this out into the world much more than the woman who is permanently concerned about her image. Pregnant or not pregnant, it's the same dilemma. Hopefully, by seven months of pregnancy onwards you will have settled into your shape and feel more comfortable in your skin. The early months are the worst time of all, as people think that you have just put on weight.

All is not lost if you've been feasting on a diet rich in cakes and chocolates. You can stop buying them from today. If they're not in your cupboard, they can't be in your stomach. Some women don't even need to be overeating to gain weight; the simple introduction of pregnancy hormones into their system is enough. There is absolutely no need to go on a strict diet. Rather, try to pay attention to the food you are putting into your mouth. Do not do anything in excess such as eating or eliminating certain foods. If you are concerned in any way by the amount of weight you are gaining, I suggest that you speak with your medical care provider.

By eating a daily diet of natural good quality food and including weekly exercise such as yoga, walking and swimming, you will ensure a healthy pregnancy for yourself. Many women, who have paid attention to what they eat and generally looked after themselves, get back into great shape soon after giving birth. Some even felt that their body, post-baby, was the best it had ever been, and this was due to the exceptional care they paid to what they ate and did during the pregnancy. A visit to a reputable nutritionist, both during and after pregnancy, is highly recommended. This will help you to remain healthy and strong and regain balance and equilibrium in your body.

Do not despair if you're feeling like your body is out of control. One thing you can still take charge of is your image. Gone are the days when mum-to-be was expected to wear dad-to-be's shirt tails. The clothes you choose and the way you style your hair can make a big impact on your self-esteem so it's worth making the effort. Your style may have changed completely, just like your taste buds. Experiment with different looks and discover the new you emerging in the mirror month by month. Remember to buy your normal size in pregnancy clothes – clothes that are big and baggy will just make you look bigger. We trick ourselves into thinking that we are able to hide away under clothes. Better to use accessories like bags and shoes as they distract your eyes away from the bits you may not like. You will be able to keep wearing these beyond the nine months too.

It's likely that you'll be shopping almost daily for everything that your baby needs — it's a shocking amount of stuff! What you're likely to forget is that you have needs too, especially after giving birth. Among other things you will need new nightwear, healing herbs and lotions and new accessories to help to brighten yourself and distract the eye and your thoughts from your post-natal stomach.

Pamper yourself and be pampered every day. Make this your daily mantra. Start by making a little extra time for yourself in the bathroom and have a relaxing bath with safe for pregnancy essential oils like lavender, neroli and mandarin. It is very important that you always cross-check any essential oils you use during your pregnancy. Many can be dangerous for you to use, particularly in the first 20 weeks. I would also advise you to check the contents of any massage oils before use. If in doubt, remember that olive oil is always the best for massaging. Alternatively, enjoy rubbing moisturising cream all over your body. Slow down so you can experience the feeling and the sheer luxury of having time to touch yourself. Cover your whole body, noticing how soft and beautiful you are in your pregnant shape. Look at yourself in the mirror and find something good about your body every day. If funds permit, have a pregnancy massage or reflexology session once a month. Always check that your practitioner has experience working with pregnancy. See the resources section for recommendations.

Look after your feet by having a pedicure. You could take it in turns with other pregnant mums to paint each other's toenails rather than meeting up in the coffee shop. You'll get more long-term satisfaction from your beautiful feet and it will be a good excuse to put them up to admire them. One husband shaved his wife's legs, washed her hair and painted her toenails from day one of her three pregnancies.

I'm glad to say that some women feel that they look wonderful during pregnancy and are captivated by their bodily changes. Becoming pregnant and growing bigger can sometimes help women to feel better about their bodies. They relish growing in size, particularly if they haven't liked their body shape before. Sometimes becoming round naturally can boost your confidence. Some women tell me that they feel at their most womanly during pregnancy. They have breasts and curves and relish wearing fitted clothes that they would normally shy away from.

♀♂ **Couple time**

To help you to celebrate your body it's worth playing around with your partner to create a beautiful photo album of your pregnant shape. So many women tell me that they wish they had taken more pictures of themselves in the last months of their pregnancy. It's a special record for you both in years to come. If this is not your first pregnancy, you'll find that no two bumps look exactly the same. Have a chat with your partner about what you would like to create. Stay within your comfort levels — nobody is forcing you to become a pregnant porn queen. With a little imagination, the inside of your house can become the backdrop for whatever tickles your fancy. Remember that this is personal between you and your partner and for this reason your photos can be as intimate and sexy as you would like. If you're feeling shy about him snapping you in the flesh, you could try varying lighting, using shadows and wearing transparent clothes that silhouette your shape. If you wear make-up, remember to put on a bit more than usual as this creates a more professional photo finish. Choose your props carefully so that they enhance your shape and hide any bits that you'd prefer to keep under wraps.

Enjoy stepping into your roles as model and photographer. Go for it – really let your hair down. Imagine that you're the hottest pregnant model in the world. Play music to get in the mood. Move your body, relax, smile and let that naughty look come through the lens. Go on, let yourself become the sexy mama in waiting that you dream to be, because you are. If you're simply not in the mood for performing, have him take a few shots. I'm sure that your eyes will shine from all the love and admiration that he's pouring through the lens towards you.

If you're still not convinced with the idea of taking photos, you could try having a mould taken of your pregnant belly or breasts. You can get a kit off the internet and do it at home. Staging this photo shoot or moulding day could be the most fun you've had together in ages – better for your libido than nursery shops or birth preparation classes. The truth is that most men can become quite bored with our pregnancy chatter. How can it be as exciting for him as it is for us? It wouldn't be unusual for him to go to work and forget that you're pregnant, especially in the early days. Try not to take this personally. Gradually as you grow he'll come on-board, especially when you bump into him and take up all the available space in the bed. The good news is that most dads find their partners more beautiful the more pregnant they become.

♂ His tip

What she needs from you in the last months of pregnancy is your support and dedication. Be around as much as possible, so she can share with you how she is feeling. Listen and compliment her on how well she's doing, how much you value her and how fantastic she looks. You'll see her blossom in front of your eyes. This will be like the most nourishing food for her soul and will help you to stay close in the last months.

Take charge of your social diary and book up a couple of surprise romantic dinners together. Plan a break away together and indulge her with your full attention. Spoil her by organising flowers in the hotel room and massage treats. Remember to pamper yourself too. You won't be so attractive if you're all rung out and stressed.

And if you can't spare the cash to get away, have a weekend lock-in at home. Make a big effort not to answer the phone or emails. You can create a romantic atmosphere with candles and music. Change the bed sheets and towels and buy a few culinary indulgences to spoil yourselves a little. You could even tell your family and friends that you are away for the weekend so that they leave you alone, but remember to take your romantic strolls away from your usual haunts.

YOUR VAGINA DURING PREGNANCY

Even though your friends and neighbours will be privy to the changes in your body shape, one thing they won't know or talk about will be the changes inside your vagina. These will be more obvious during the last couple of months as the hormones that stretch everything out increase. It's not only your hips that are getting wider but the internal dimensions of your vagina too. The tissues on the inside and the outside have literally ripened. They may look, feel and taste completely different. Just like soft fruit ripens, so the inside of your vagina will be thicker and swollen and the colour will change from shades of pale pink and red to violet and purple as a result of the increased blood supply. If this sounds like how your vagina feels when you're sexually aroused, then you'll be right. It can feel like you're in a permanent state of gentle sexual arousal. Even if you've not been particularly sexually active through the last months, you will have noticed the different feelings down there. With the extra pressure on the genital organs and an increase in vaginal lubrication, some women say they literally feel juicy all day.

Have a look at your genitals in a hand-held mirror and see for yourself if you've changed during pregnancy. You may see a completely different you. This can come as a reminder to go to the beauty salon for a pre-birth wax and tidy up. Sit with your legs open at the edge of the bed. Slip forward and hold the mirror at an angle and slightly below and away from your genital area. What you'll be looking at is technically called the vulva, the name given to your external sex organs. You'll see two sets of lips (or labia): the outer lips that are covered in hair and are easily visible and the inner lips that are normally concealed by the outer pair, although they may be larger and more visible during pregnancy. Gently pop your finger between the lips and practice squeezing the pelvic floor muscles around your finger. See how tight these muscles are today and know that they will return to this state, or even better following the birth, with a little daily effort. Like all muscles in your body, they need to be exercised regularly.

Late Pregnancy

Start today by contracting your pelvic floor muscles and build up to 100 per day. To feel these muscles, stop mid-flow as you're urinating and you will feel them contracting and releasing as you continue to flow. Imagine that you are gathering together a circle of muscles inside your vagina, like you are pulling up the strings to close a drawstring bag. This is the contraction, and letting go of the string releases them. There are so many benefits for your health in working these muscles, especially for your sex life. It's a worthwhile habit to have and not just during pregnancy. Put up a fridge magnet that reminds you to squeeze ten times whenever you see it.

It's easy to lose sight of your genital area as being anything but a birth canal in the last months of pregnancy. It's likely that you've literally lost sight of it under your bump by now too. Midwives and birth educators encourage you to think practically about your vagina. Perineal massage, which involves massaging the perineum (the area between the anus and the vagina) with oil has by now replaced foreplay. Statistics show that doing this could help prevent tearing of the perineum during labour. Having said this, please do your perineal massage from 20 weeks and stretching the vagina from 35 weeks. See the resources section for more tips on how to do this. But has your midwife told you how important a loving sexual relationship is for the well-being of the pregnancy? Whenever you become sexually aroused, you release oxytocin into your bloodstream. This is sometimes called the happiness hormone and helps to tone up the uterus. Now that's a good result and a great reason to be sexual.

♂ **His tip**

Many couples enjoy sharing a perineal massage together. It will help you to prepare for the birth and your partner will welcome your involvement. Some women are shy to do this at first but with a little reassurance and encouragement from you, they are able to overcome this.

Sometimes it is difficult to verbalise our emotions; potentially we look away from our deepest fears and we often don't even know they exist until one day they rear their ugly heads, usually in the most inappropriate ways and situations. I have seen many pregnant mums overcome stubborn emotions or negative thoughts by having a creative outlet, such as working with clay. See the resources section for more information on this.

YOUR SEX DRIVE DURING PREGNANCY

Watch out. It's not unusual for women to become more sexually excited during the last weeks of their pregnancy, even if they have had little interest up till then. The uterus becomes particularly sensitive to oxytocin at this time and can lead to spontaneous labour. On the other hand, some women have a very high libido throughout pregnancy and will notice increased orgasmic responsiveness, perhaps even multiple orgasms. Nothing can be considered normal and this is most baffling for men. In our non-pregnant state, our sexual appetites will change throughout the month. Sexual preferences in pregnancy can be like a roller-coaster ride. One mum explained to me that literally everything that she had liked to do sexually before pregnancy, she could no longer do. However, in the last weeks, she wanted to have lots of sex, which worked well for her partner until she had a show following intercourse. He then flatly refused to 'go down there again' until after the baby was born. She had been following her instincts about what would bring the baby on and she delivered soon after.

There are no rules about sexual response during pregnancy. Some women want it more, some less and some not at all. Fortunately, these days we have more factual information about the massive increase in sex hormones. By the time of delivery, progesterone has increased to 25 times its pre-pregnancy norm. Both oestrogen and progesterone are suspected of lowering sexual desire, though they also increase the blood supply to the pelvic area and can make women feel an increased need for release of sexual tension.

Meanwhile, the mother's androgen (male hormone) levels rise progressively throughout pregnancy, perhaps counter-acting the sexual depressant effects of progesterone and oestrogen.

Whether you're hot to trot or completely off it, sexuality during pregnancy should always take into account what is safe and what is comfortable. Obviously if a woman doesn't desire sex it won't be comfortable. She should never be forced into doing something she doesn't want to do, especially if she feels that it is her duty. It's just as important during pregnancy as at any other time, to have some reason of your own to engage in sex, something that is for you both.

Tell your partner how you are feeling sexually. Try to say it without blaming him or yourself. Drop the guilt. You may be feeling sensations differently and your energy would be best used in exploring what types of contact would give you the most satisfaction. You might suggest that you try to increase your daily kissing and cuddling quota. It's easy to forget about this important way of communicating together. He may be feeling too shy to tell you that he fancies you more than ever now that you're pregnant. Even if you don't feel like participating with him, let him know that his desires are not wrong but that they are his responsibility not yours. One man explained to me that his partner's pregnant shape turned him on. Her increasing size made her more of a woman and more sexy. Fortunately for this couple, her libido grew with her.

Sexual intimacy doesn't have to include intercourse and being physical with each other doesn't have to lead to anything other than a good night's sleep. It may be difficult to get into your usual cuddle position in bed so try to adapt it so that he can cuddle you from behind, as you lie on your side with your supporting pillows out front. If sleeping together becomes too difficult as you keep waking him up to go to the loo, then increase the cuddles you have on the sofa before bedtime. Sometimes our fear of the expectation that any physical contact must lead to intercourse is the reason why a lot of people give up on cuddles. We all need lots of cuddles, it's human nature and especially so for the mum-to-be.

♂ **His tip**

Don't take anything she says about sex personally. If she thinks that you smell or taste bad, remember that her senses to keep the baby safe are acute during pregnancy. If she doesn't like French kissing because she has excess saliva in her mouth, remember that extra lubrication isn't only vaginal. And if she doesn't want you to touch (or see) her breasts, remember that they may be three times their usual size and feel like melons to her. Go with it.

♀♂ **Couple time**

Give each other a back and shoulder massage with a pregnancy massage oil (see resources for some recommendations). Do this at least once a week. Make it into a special occasion and choose an appropriate time of day when you're least tired. Light candles and play relaxing music. All sensual touch will remind you both that you are still lovers. Experiment with different stokes and pressure. Try to flow your movements in an upward direction as this will also help with lymphatic drainage and keep you feeling less bloated in the final months. Don't limit yourselves to just touching with your hands. Introduce your full body – your feet, mouth, breasts – and play with feathers, rounded stones and sensual materials. Remember to ask each other for feedback about your technique. Practice makes perfect.

Touching each other keeps you physically intimate, not only when libido is low, but also when any issues of safety may preclude intercourse. Research about the safety of sex during pregnancy is inconclusive but by the third trimester, you should know if sex poses any possible risk to either you or the baby.

Lovers tip

Try putting the penis into the vagina without thrusting. Use plenty of lubrication. Encourage her to squeeze and release her pelvic muscles around you. Stay for as long as feels comfortable for you both. Move on to other things or simply stop and cuddle each other whilst you talk about how it felt.

Alternatively, experiment with soft penetration. This means 'inserting' his soft penis into your vagina. Don't be afraid to take him in your hands and push him inside you. This is an excellent technique if you don't particularly want to have 'normal' intercourse but still desire physical intimacy. It is best to try this after he has ejaculated.

Many men in particular are concerned about the safety of the baby during this time and tell me that this is the main reason that they go off having sex with their partners, particularly at term. They feel that their penis is too close to the baby's head during intercourse and avoid anything too strenuous or too noisy, particularly after six months when we're told that the foetus can hear. Remember that even when the baby is fully engaged in the pelvis, the soft tissues of the cervix and the amnitoic fluid will protect him from harm, acting as a cushion, not to mention soundproofing.

Many women will love the freedom of not having to use birth control but this may not be enough to sway him from seeing you as an untouchable mother figure. One man noticed how his libido had dropped even before he knew that his partner was pregnant. Somehow he found himself thinking 'that she looked like someone's mother.' It's tricky if you're hot and horny and he is reluctant but you can only accept that the way he feels is complex and not personal.

Keep open the channels of communication between you and your partner. I know that it's hard but try not to nag him or to pull back your affections. Stay in there. He may begin to open up with you and as he feels lighter in his heart, he may get more aroused. In the meantime continue to engage with your own pleasure through masturbation, if that was what you did before pregnancy. In a healthy pregnancy this will do nothing but be of benefit to the development of the baby. Your partner will probably feel relieved that you are taking care of your own sexual needs and be happier to engage in cuddles without the anxiety that you may try for sex with him. If you're feeling unusually sexually frustrated, consider learning to masturbate. See the resources section for further tips on how to do this.

Late Pregnancy

Overall, couples tend to come to natural solutions to any sexual complications that are brought on by the increasing size of late pregnancy. This is especially the case when it comes to the choice of positions for intercourse. I recommend that you experiment with 'her on top' positions. Straddle him with your back as straight as you can. This position is ideal for allowing you to be in control of the pace and depth of penetration. Be aware that if you have leaking breasts then this position will definitely cause you to spray your partner. To avoid this, wear a sexy bra with hidden breast pads. Also consider experimenting with 'from behind' positions, with either him lying behind you as you both lie on your sides or you on all fours. Encourage him to reach his hands around to pleasure your clitoris and nipples. You'll need to increase the supply of pillows and cushions for extra support and remember to raise her head and shoulders to avoid heartburn and indigestion which, after the fifth month, come from lying flat.

If you go over your dates then you'll usually be advised to go home and have lots of sex. You're told that sex can start labour and that sperm can act as a trigger for the labour. Basically, the highest natural concentration of prostaglandins is found in semen. If you go to hospital for a formal induction, you may have a pessary of prostaglandins inserted into the vagina close to the cervix. Before you get to this stage it's worth trying the natural way – sperm from your own partner.

Lovers tip

Try it this way to bring on the birth: She lies on her back with her head and shoulders well supported. He kneels between her open legs and gently places her legs over his shoulders. He enters so that his penis tip can touch the cervix. This is an extremely deep position and may not be particularly comfortable or pleasurable for her, so it would be best for both of you to be really aroused by mutual stimulation and lots of nipple sucking before he enters. This will avoid him over-thrusting. If she manages to achieve orgasm, this will also increase the release of oxytocin, which has been known to trigger spontaneous orgasms. Once he ejaculates he should stay inside for around 5 minutes and she should keep her legs raised for up to 15 minutes to give the semen every chance of coating the cervix. Thanks to Mother Nature, the more aroused she is, the more her cervix will dip into the seminal fluid. Enjoy a gentle cuddle together before drifting off to sleep. Getting rest is important in case you are woken with contractions during the night.

BIRTH

However it happens, however long it takes or wherever you are, the impact of giving birth will be with you always. It is the most momentous and life-changing event that we can ever experience. However, as I am not in the business of writing a book about the process of birth but about the impact it has on your sex life and intimacy, I will resist the temptation to indulge. Instead, I will leave it to the likes of Sheila Kitzinger, Gowri Motha and Yehudi Gordon, to name but a few, to make this worthwhile contribution to your bookshelves.

It may seem startling to some of you to even consider that the process of childbirth could be remotely sexual, especially as this concept is never introduced into antenatal classes. But considering that the central focus of childbirth is in the pelvis and that all the feelings of contracting uterine muscles, of the fanning open of the cervix and soft tissues and the descending baby, pour through the genitals, it is not so far-fetched. The depending factor will be how you interpret these feelings and the circumstances in which you give birth. It doesn't necessarily follow that your birth experience will relate to your everyday sexual experience. In this way you may have low sexual appetite and find yourself filled with the most intense sexual feelings throughout birth and vice versa. Some women dance with abandon through every contraction and experience sexual surges as strong as orgasms. Others may feel nothing. It's just as confusing and unpredictable as the libido throughout pregnancy. One mum told me that she felt aroused throughout her labour, but moments before delivery, she had an intense surge of libido. She grabbed her partner around his head and kissed him with wanton passion. Neither of them had experienced such a full-on kiss before and it shocked and overwhelmed him. They have since had many laughs together about this.

If you've previously had a difficult birth in which you felt distressed and trapped, you may be struggling to equate sexual feelings with giving birth. Obviously the more physically exhausted you feel and the amount of medical intervention you have will impact the natural flow of birthing hormones. But there is still the possibility that it will happen, if we let it. Giving birth is about letting go; it's about being deeply relaxed, whatever the circumstances and letting the unexpected happen. And even if it didn't and you just can't allow yourself to believe that it will, why not allow yourself to consider that it might.

A word of caution to any of you who have experienced sexual abuse in your life or had memories of abuse surfacing following previous births — take care of yourself and refer to the resources section if you require further help. One lady told me of her two very different birth experiences. A victim of childhood incest, her first experience of childbirth was very long and complicated; she had an episiotomy and many bad memories. Following the birth she had difficulty bonding with her baby and had to be re-stitched on numerous occasions. Before her second birth she began to consider how her sexuality had and could impact on her experience of birth; she worked hard on her childhood memories. After she delivered her second baby naturally in water with no damage to her perineum, she described to me that she felt the memories of incest leaving her body with the final push. This is a great story of self-empowerment and healing.

How your partner is affected by the birth will have a big impact on your own experience. You must think ahead about how you as a couple would like to proceed. These days quite a number of women tell me that they would prefer their partners not to be present in the delivery room. This is a radical change from the last 30 years. Given the choice, these women would prefer to have the support of a female birthing partner, such as a 'doula' or labour support person (see resources). Often they feel unable to tell their partners that this is how they feel, for fear of hurting their feelings. Childbirth guru Michel Odent believes that some men, in their anxiety for the woman, try to talk rationally to her, but by doing so they distract her and pass on their own fear. Women, he says, may be better off giving birth accompanied by another woman who has had a child. Despite this advice, around 90 per cent of all fathers are present at the births of their children. There is still a pressure put on men to be there, even if it's the last place they would like be. However, for most men, seeing their child born is one of the highest points of their lives — something that they would never want to miss at any cost.

♀♂ Couple time

Most of you will have written a birth plan by now. If not I would strongly recommend that you take a couple of hours to sit down together and do this. You will want to include your hopes, dreams and wishes for how you would like the birth to be. Most midwives will always do their utmost to help you to achieve these. If this is your first child, it may be difficult to know how you will feel, but try to discuss obvious concerns. Listen to each other's point of view and don't take it personally. Ultimately she should have the final say about what she wants. Decide where he will be for the birth, in the room or outside and get agreement about where he will stand for the delivery and any vaginal examinations or interventions. Do you want photos or a DVD taken during the birth or afterwards? If so, establish the rules for the camera or recorder. Give him a list of jobs — men like to have something to do, especially as childbirth can be very out of control. Make a job list together so you both are clear what is expected.

The biggest concern that women have about their partners being at the birth is that they will see too much. They also worry that their partners will find the sight of childbirth so frightening that they may be put off having sex with them forever. Some men feel uncomfortable with their partner's physical exposure, especially if a male doctor is examining her. In contrast, other men find that seeing her involved in such a powerful experience enhances their sexual feelings towards her. Birth is an unpredictable event just like our reactions to it. One man saw his wife give birth three times and each time he subsequently lost his sexual desire. On the fourth time he saw her give birth he found it to be a sexual experience and saw her as a goddess. They are now enjoying their sex life. We can learn so much from this wonderful story. Firstly, if he hadn't been to birth number four, he would never have had this transforming and healing sexual experience. Secondly, it was the position in which she delivered, on all fours that made the difference for him. He couldn't see directly into her vagina, which he had on the previous three occasions. Bravo to them and their children.

Decide how you feel about him seeing your vagina, intervention and all during childbirth. If this bothers you today, it certainly will during labour. If you are worried about this, write in your birth plan that you do not want him to be down below during labour but at head height and to the side. Maybe it is important to you to be covered up to retain your dignity. This is your right and the midwives and obstetricians will respect this. If you are indifferent about the question, do this too. It is up to you to decide how much you tell him about your reasons for this. The mystique of your genitals will remain intact for you both. If you feel completely relaxed about him seeing everything, that's great. Be aware that birth holds its surprises and you don't want this to be one of them.

It's not your job to take care of him or what he sees in the labour room. It's his responsibility to stick to the agreements that you have made together. One woman was so concerned about her partner seeing her in a compromised position, that she confused the feeling of her baby's head dropping into the birth canal with wanting to empty her bowels. Her stress and panic about the possibility of him seeing her going to the toilet 'in public' overrode her inner connection with the process of the birth and as a result she held back and delayed the final stage of labour. Conversely, pushing out her son would have been an easier option because he knew that she wanted him at her head end for this. Good communication prior to the birth is vital. In this case, Dad could have left the room briefly for her to empty her bowels in private at which point she would have relaxed and realised that the baby was coming.

———————————

The best outcome for the couple that share the birth is that it creates a stronger bond between them and with the baby. When both partners have a well-defined role to play, the process of birth can run smoothly. It will be an immense help to know each other's hopes, dreams and desires.

Don't panic in these last weeks – there are several things that can help you get through this momentous time. Firstly, calmness is the best tool you could wish for. A sense of humour is the second, especially if you can share with your nearest and dearest. Communication is the third. Non-verbal communication, body language and gestures between the two of you will deepen your intimacy too. Your relationship is a private affair and no matter how much the outside world tries to interfere with their doom and gloom stories, these last weeks are your precious time. You're going on an adventure together and like any explorers you need time for all the Rs: rest, relaxation, reconnaissance and remembering why you got together in the first place. Enjoy this time together and remember it's not the end but the beginning of a new and exciting chapter in your lives together.

♂ **His tip**

If you have any concerns about being at the birth, it's a good idea to talk it through with other men who have had the same experience. You need to be able to talk about your fears and concerns, especially if you are squeamish or worried that it will impact the way you feel about her sexually.

Decide what you think is important to share with her and think about how you will say it. Remember that she will be super sensitive in the last months of the pregnancy so choose your words carefully.

Whatever she decides on is the right decision. She must have the final say about what she wants to happen at the birth. If this upsets you, say so but try not to argue or criticise her. Usually it's not personal.

Be open-minded. This is a good approach to parenting together. Be flexible – expect the unexpected. She may change her mind during the birth so try to go with it.

2

Month One

I wish that I could give you a rubber-stamp guarantee of how you'll be feeling after giving birth, but I can't, as every birth is unique, just like we are. I have listened to literally thousands of birth stories over the years and I can tell you that no two parents' experiences have ever been the same. I could fill a whole page with superlatives describing the experience and you may still not find yours. There are simply no rules. This can be reassuring for some and downright annoying for others. You may have had a good, drug-free birth and be feeling elated or a birth pumped full of drugs and high-tech action and be feeling rung out. The best news is that the pure joy and love that you feel when you hold your newborn for the first time is enough to lift you up and away. It can carry you along for days, weeks and even months following the birth. This is the experience that most of us share.

However you gave birth, it's vital to celebrate this wonderful achievement. Having a baby is an amazing act of power and whether you had a natural or assisted birth, nothing should detract from this fact. As you move into these early days of being parents, there's work to be done healing, recovering and recreating yourselves into new, vibrant and sexy parents. I'm referring to both of you here, although it's Mum who needs the immediate attention to help her physical recovery. I can already hear you wondering how you will ever find the time to look after yourself now that you have a little extra person who needs you 24/7. So let's get clear straight away that, at the beginning of your new life, you must make yourself a priority. Your appearance, your desires, feelings and dreams are just as important today as they were before you gave birth. There's nothing in the motherhood rule book to state that you should come last in the pecking order. It may feel like this today, after you have surrendered your body for the nourishment, development and safe delivery of another human being for the best part of a year. Yes, you did this as an act of love but it's a vast service and you deserve time to recover and to enjoy getting to know the new you.

TAKE TIME FOR YOU

Self-pleasure is a phrase that we don't often read in guide-books for new mums. There are plenty of references to exhaustion and pain in the early weeks and more exhaustion and resentment in the following months. Maternal guilt begins with last push and is infinite. So does this information make us feel good? I don't think so. It's time to challenge these beliefs and you are the only one who can do this. In simple terms, you literally make your own bed from day one and have no choice but to lie in it. If you have already made a public statement on the maternity ward that you no longer have the time to wash, fix your hair, put a bit of lipstick on and clean your teeth, then who can blame the world for believing that this is the status quo for you as a mum?

Ensure that you clean your teeth, brush your hair, take a bath/wash down and wear your best nightwear as soon after giving birth as you can and certainly before anyone visits. If you wear make-up, put on a little blusher and mascara to give your face some colour and depth. Spend about 15 minutes grooming yourself – this will help you to feel good when you look back at the first-day photos. Ask Dad or a caring midwife to give you time to be on your own to look in the mirror at the new you. Be kind to yourself.

If you're reading this before delivery or if it's your second or subsequent child, discuss this scenario with your partner in advance and get his agreement that this will happen. Write it into your birth plan to be sure. You may not believe this but nobody can prepare you for the struggle and near fight you will have for this 'you' time. Many forces are working against you; some may be home-made, such as hormones and lack of sleep, and others man-made – people's opinions about how you should behave as a mother will be endless. It's up to you to decide what your priorities are. It's also up to you to make sure that you get time for you every day, no matter what. You will need to design your day so that you find time for yourself. It may be during a short nap time (it is not true that babies never ever sleep), when Dad or Granny is on hand or when you hire someone to help you.

Time for you is not a luxury. It is an absolute necessity. It is not time to clean the kitchen, vacuum the house or dash to the supermarket. It is time for you to pamper yourself a little, lie in the bath with safe essential oils and herbs, style your hair, file and paint your nails, meditate and anything else that makes you feel emotionally and mentally good. Even though you may doubt that your body and genitals will ever return to *normal,* you can still take care of the bits that you see with your clothes on. If you can afford it, have a beauty therapist or hairdresser visit you at home – you can breastfeed while you have a blow-dry. Even though you feel and may well look exhausted, this will raise your spirits and your sparkle for a short burst. Little and often is key here.

Have hand cream in the kitchen, bedroom and living room so you can get to it whenever you have a spare second. The same goes with body lotion to soothe any dry bits. Why should it be just your baby who gets all the luxurious products? Simply fit your pampering into your new timetable. It only takes a minute to rub cream into your hands but the feelings of pleasure will stay with you for hours, if you let them.

SOOTHING YOUR BODY AFTER BIRTH

In the early days and weeks, your 'you' time will be focused on the recovery of any bits of your body that feel like they have been at war. There are many natural remedies to help with healing and I recommend further reading in the resources section. Try to find yourself a qualified homeopath and cranial osteopath before you give birth – it's worth a visit so they can get to know you while you are pregnant. They will then only be a phone call away should you need them in these early weeks after giving birth.

Even though all birth stories are different, most women share similar post-natal times:

'I feel like my body has been run over by a bus.'

Whatever your experience of birth, your body will benefit from taking homeopathy. These days, the following remedies are commonplace and can be found in your local chemist. As with all natural remedies they must be treated as medication and I advise you to read the contraindications. It's a good idea to take Arnica 200 straight after the birth, especially if you had a Caesarean. All new mums can benefit from taking hyperium 200 as well as arnica several times a day for the first three to five days after having the baby.

'My perineum and vagina are so painful and swollen.'

Bathing in a special perineum healing herbal mix will help to sort this out. See the resources section for more information on where to buy this. Alternatively you can brew a pot of chamomile tea and pour the steeped contents into your bath. Relax in the water for 20 minutes to really benefit from the tea's soothing properties.

'My bottom feels like it is about to fall out.'

Try a homeopathic topical cream for haemorrhoid relief.

'It feels so bruised I can't sit down.'

You could apply an ice pack for ten minutes, three times a day whilst lying down. You could also bathe your perineum with cotton swabs soaked in a solution of 50ml of water containing ten to twenty drops of the mother tincture calendula.

'I'm too frightened to poo – I might burst my stitches.'

When you open your bowels, place a clean sanitary pad either against your Caesarean scar or episiotomy on the perineum and apply gentle support to the wound. Relax and visualise your bowels opening without strain.

'It stings, every time I wee.'

Add lemon or cranberry juice to your drinking water to alkalise your urine. You could also pour tepid chamomile tea or the healing infusion, between your legs and down the toilet as you go.

'My breasts feel like they are about to burst.'

Put cabbage leaves in the fridge then put them into your feeding bra.

'My nipples are so sore they're starting to bleed.'

Finely grate carrots and refrigerate them. Put them on to a cotton pad and place over your nipple inside your bra.

'I feel low and exhausted.'

It's natural to feel this way during the first days and weeks. More than half of all mothers experience feeling tired, anxious, weepy or desperate. Try to take a daily bath with two drops of geranium oil and spend a few moments visualising yourself swaddled in a soft pink blanket. Allow yourself to feel its softness and comfort and safety. Massage yourself with a blend of Rose Otto essential oil and olive oil. Even if you can only manage to rub it into your neck and arms, hands and legs it will benefit you immensely. Rose Otto oil can really lift your mood.

POST-NATAL DEPRESSION (PND)

If you are experiencing extreme lows or highs and feeling despondent or even suicidal, I urge you to tell your GP or health visitor. It's important that you don't keep it a secret, and please do not feel guilty about how you are feeling, especially if you are having negative feelings towards your baby. Post-natal depression is an imbalance of the brain chemistry. It's not your fault. One mum described her experience of post-natal depression in such detail and I feel that it is valuable for us all to share this with her. We hear so little about post-natal depression, it seems to be a well-kept, even hidden, secret and this is not good. The more we tell each other the truth, the more we can empower other mums to do the same.

The difference between post-natal depression and baby blues is easy to spot. With baby blues you feel sad, disappointed, despairing even; you feel that this baby business isn't what you expected. However, these feelings are fairly short-term and usually last from a few days to a few weeks. With post-natal depression you feel all of the above but 100 times worse, to the point where you may feel like rejecting and even hurting your baby. You have a sense that you have nothing inside yourself to meet the baby's needs, which often produces side-effects of acute anxiety.

♂ **His tip**

Pay close attention to your partner's behaviour after she has given birth. Look out for symptoms such as despondency, panic, guilt, exhaustion and not wanting to feed or care for the baby or herself. If you feel at all concerned that your partner has post-natal depression, go and talk to your GP for advice. Never underestimate the impact that this level of responsibility has on you; you may feel helpless and scared and will definitely benefit from sharing this information with your doctor. Research post-natal depression on the internet and you'll read countless stories that are similar to your own. But don't delay recognising what is staring you in the face like many dads before you have. Sorry to be so hard line but you will be helping her by telling your GP, you're not reporting that she is a bad mother. If you refuse her help because of your own pride, I guarantee you that this will cause long term damage to your relationship. She may lose trust in your ability to take care of her in the future.

Post-natal depression is not just depression; it's an illness that requires a course of anti-depressants. This mum went straight to her GP as soon as she felt the urge to throw her daughter against the wall when she cried. A course of antidepressants for 18 months got her through, but despite having support from her partner, it was a lonely road with feelings of horrendous guilt. She feels better now, three and a half years on, and has now completely bonded with her daughter.

ASKING FOR HELP

Help is always available if we allow it to be. Asking for help from people, including your own partner, can be challenging and accepting it may be devastating to your self-esteem. Until a few months ago, you were your own woman, in charge of your own life, and you probably never needed to ask permission to do or have anything. Try to break this pattern and begin to ask for help from your partner, parents, siblings, friends and neighbours. In some societies new mums are supported by their community with cooking, cleaning and help with shopping. If all else fails, pay for extra help. You'll look back and realise that it was money well spent – a cost to your purse rather than your own energy. I believe that you can never have enough help in these early weeks. Every time you pass on a chore to someone else you will gain energy. Remember only to leave your baby with a trusted

the best role model you can give to your children, too.

How can you ever envisage making time for your partner and your relationship, without firstly making time for you? A car can't run without petrol. Likewise, you can only give to a relationship, especially sexually, if you've had some juice for yourself. One mum told me that after she had recovered from the initial shock of the responsibility of her new baby, she gathered her strength and strode forward. She realised that this 'thing' called motherhood was totally her responsibility. After all, she had chosen it, and only she could make it work for her. This positive approach is very empowering for us all. We constantly waste energy complaining about the exhaustion and I am certain that this increases fatigue. It's a vicious circle. Be aware that moaning and groaning can become an integral part of post-natal groups too. Sharing the pitfalls with old friends or your partner could prove to be the better option.

This concept may come as a shock to you, but the reality is that you and your partner are in this baby thing together. Life hasn't just changed for you; it's changed for him too and for your relationship dynamic. It is more important now than ever that you keep your channels of communication open. You will have a lot to talk about and to share on your journey as parents. Before you began your family, you probably chatted in the evenings and weekends about your fears, hopes and dreams. Even if you weren't big talkers, you would have shared the language of lovemaking. That's how you got here. But this very private, intimate way of communicating is taking a short siesta — at the very least in these early weeks — so talking together will keep you linked as lovers and will reduce confrontation down the line.

COMMUNICATION

There are three simple rules of communication: when, where and how. When is about choosing a good time to talk, for example not when you are both dog-tired. There will be a time that suits you both but you will need to search for it beyond your excuses. This takes effort from you both but it's worth it — honestly. Try not to talk about issues while they are happening. Talking about the quality of the washing-up or the ironing, for instance, rubber gloves on or iron in your hand, will not go down too well and could be dangerous.

Where you speak to each other is also important. You need to be able to give each other your attention so, in front of the television isn't a great choice. Nor is in bed, as you will probably fall asleep. The bedroom is certainly not the place to talk about your sex life either.

Finally, how you speak to each other, the tone you use or how loud your voice is will affect the impact of what you have to say. Frustrations, resentment and jealousy are easy to spot. Nobody will want to listen to you mouthing off. Calm down, walk away and agree to discuss your upsets a few hours or a day later (not years later).

> ♀♂ **Couple tip**
>
> Laughter is a great healer in relationships, especially when you feel the heat coming on between the two of you. Try to see the funny side of life. If you step back for a moment you will see that much of what you do together as parents in the early weeks makes excellent slapstick. Imagine if you were the fly on the wall watching you change your first nappy or pushing the pram up steps for the first time.

It's vital that you have time to talk to each other without being distracted by your baby. Plan this for when your baby is certain to be asleep. You need to snatch opportunities in these early months for everything from the shopping, cleaning and tidying to your own time for yourself and for your partner.

One couple were taken by surprise several months after the birth when they settled down together for a romantic meal and decided to put on a relaxing CD. They pressed play but had forgotten that it was the CD they had used for the birth and as they began to listen to it they started to cry and remember all the bad memories they hadn't spoken about previously. Fortunately, they found this was a valuable way

♀♂ **Couple time**

Choose a time when your baby is asleep and talk to each other about your memories of the birth: what you saw, felt and heard. Be honest with each other. Remember to say how you are truly feeling in these early days/weeks.

Listen without interrupting each other as this gives you a better chance to delve into your memory banks. It may seem like a lifetime ago or just five minutes before that you gave birth. When your partner has finished speaking, ask questions and say how you are feeling too. Remind each other of how proud you are of one another. You are embarking on a massive journey together. To finish, have a great big cuddle. If your baby wakes up during this, which the little darlings have a habit of doing, especially when you get physical together, then let your baby join in – babies love to cuddle too.

Couples will often cry, then laugh, then cry again when they talk about the birth of their child. It's quite normal to experience this range of emotions. You have shared the most incredible and powerful event together. By simply talking about this, with open hearts, you will become closer. It's possible that your partner will be able to fill in any missing pieces from the birth that you may have forgotten. In the case of one mum, it helped her to believe that she had actually given birth, as she delivered so quickly. Who else is willing to listen to your war and glory stories? Who else will love you more for being there through it all? If you are having flashbacks or particular recurring issues from the birth, you may need to talk it through again and again.

of releasing and sharing their experience. With their second child, they talked about the birth within days of being home. They listened to each other and Mum in particular felt better about the birth as she listened to Dad telling her how well she had done. If you find that these memories just won't go away or if they remind you of anything negative that has happened to you before, then seek professional help right away. See the resources for more information.

Becoming a new family requires a time of adjustment. It can sometimes take you up until the first month and longer after birth to come to terms with the change in your lifestyle. It isn't simply the relationship with your partner that has changed but much of what you consider to be 'normal' aspects of life will have undergone a 180 degree turn. Things such as popping down the shop or spontaneously going out in the evening are no longer possible now that you have to look after your baby 24 hours a day, 7 days a week. There's no reason to despair; rather, you should mourn what has passed, embrace the changes and enjoy where you are today.

———————————————

Having a good time with their offspring is key to successful bonding for dads. Although in the first few weeks you may be handing the little one over to him with gritted teeth, there'll be big rewards for all of you. It will raise your self-esteem as parents and most of all increase how much you value and respect each other as parents. It's also wonderful for your child to spend time with you both. Having the opportunity to bond in these early weeks with both parents is invaluable. Try not to fall into the trap of undermining each other's parenting contribution, especially as the days and nights become longer. When we are tired and stressed we nag more and this will hurt your precious relationship.

———————————————

So how is it that you can be on such a roller coaster of emotions – plunging from the most blissed-out love spaces to the darkest thought spaces within seconds? Well, it seems to be part and parcel of parenting together. Over time, you will come to

♂ **His tip**

Even if you choose not to attend the birth, you may still have been there to share the early joy-filled moments of your child's life. But you might like to invite any birth partner/doula to paint the picture of the birth along with your partner.

Now is the perfect time to give Mum a gift to show your love and gratitude. One of the most generous gifts you could give to a new mum is to take care of the house during these early weeks to give her a break. If this sounds stressful then you'd be right. Remember that you don't have to do everything yourself. Begin the preparation and planning in the last months of the pregnancy, as your mind will be much clearer without unbroken sleep. This could include making lists of all the weekly jobs that need to be done in the house, contacting any potential help and asking your partner what she may like to eat after birth. This is of course a million dollar question as it's most likely that she will change her mind frequently in response to her body's needs and desires. Be patient and expect everything to change.

The chances are high that you will have to wrestle her out of the kitchen and demand that she puts her feet up. This will be a win-win situation for you as you learn how peaceful it is to cook solo in the kitchen. You'll also gain superstar status with every meal that you cook. Believe it or not, it's still unusual in this day and age to hear about a man who takes total charge of the house for the first few weeks after his partner has given birth. One mum told me how her post-natal group was stunned to silence when she told them of her husband's domestic fortitude. From this reaction, she began to think that there was something wrong with their relationship. I challenge you to change this and make your fellow men on the sofa the odd ones out.

Even though equality of the sexes has come on leaps and bounds over the last two decades, people will still stop and stare at a dad out on the street with his newborn child. They will be almost awestruck to see him wearing a baby sling in the supermarket and amazed to see him pushing a pram around the park on his own. He is a big attraction on the street and I hope that he is awake and alert enough to enjoy all the attention he gets. It's just the way it should be. Dads need extra time with their babies to bond, just as much as mums need their time alone. Now that's a lucky coincidence.

accept it and learn to alter your behaviour to compensate for it. In preparation, consider this very lifelike scenario:

Resentment snakes through Mum's day at home, getting bigger and more venomous around the time that Dad arrives back. She sees how easy his day was in comparison to hers and now he even has the audacity to want to speak to her. How dare he. Dad arrives home ever hopeful of a loving welcome from his partner. Instead she hands him the baby and a job list with green smoke coming out of her ears. Quick as a flash, he begins to resent her. How could she be so unwelcoming? Does she not know what a hard day he has had in comparison to hers? And she hasn't even tidied up. How could he have been demoted from being her lover to a handyman is a few short weeks?

Neither of them is right or wrong to feel the way they do, so drop the guilt if you thought that this was you I was describing. All it takes are small steps to change this from happening to you.

If he comes home from a hard day at work, try to listen to him without interrupting his story even if you find it difficult to understand or sympathise with his problems. They may seem lightweight after a day with your baby but remember that he simply wants to be listened to and validated. He is doing a fantastic job as a man, providing for his family, and it's perfectly natural that he should want to tell you about his day. Everyone can spare five minutes to listen to each other so set the timer and don't interrupt. He'll be more inclined to give you what you need if you do.

♀♂ **Couple tip**

Whether you are both new to this parenting game or even if this is not your first child, there will always be something new to learn about the journey you are embarking on together. Try to de-clutter your lives in these early weeks so you can focus on how well you are both doing.

I recommend that you take a 'babymoon'. This is a period of time following the birth when you close up shop to visitors and spend time together as your new family unit. When you are not being asked to make 1001 cups of tea by your guests, you will have more energy to get stuck into parenting and hopefully have some laughs along the way. Warn your family before the birth if this is what you are planning – it's better to get all the arguments and guilt out of the way upfront. You will also be giving a very powerful message to the world by doing this: you are saying how highly you value your relationship. It won't be long before Dad has to return to work. The time will fly by and you will have precious memories of being together and to adjusting to your new rhythm of life.

Give him permission to treat you from time to time. Trust that he knows what to do and that your baby will be in the best hands too. Let go of responsibilities for now.

Let him take charge of organising your special bath time. Water has a great capacity to heal. You can feel like you're merging with it; in reality you almost are as we're over 50 per cent water. Water also creates interesting patterns and reflections and this can be particularly relaxing as you look down into it. It's an ideal way to look at your body, especially in these early weeks when looking naked into the mirror may be too confrontational.

It's easy to forget that you have any other body parts outside your breasts for feeding and arms for baby carrying. Reach down and touch yourself through the water. Enjoy the pleasant sensations and, if you have a shower attachment, let the water spray out across your breasts, tummy, arms and legs. Even though you may feel physically exhausted, your body can't resist these sensual pulsations. Take your time to dry your whole body with the soft fresh towels and gently massage yourself with the post-natal blend of oils listed in the resources section.

Few new mums would describe this quiet time spent alone in the bath as anything other than pure pleasure. It's rare in these early days to get physical time alone. And it is a stark contrast from the feelings of intense loneliness that many mums describe, being at home every day with their family. Or in bed in the dark of the night feeding their baby whilst their partner sleeps through. It's not surprising that this new mum might feel lonely, as the career girl she knew herself to be has gone on vacation and the mother she is becoming, is still new on the block. Sometimes it can feel like she has been cast adrift in a wild sea and that she is struggling to keep herself afloat and to keep her head above water long enough to see the rock that could be most help to her now. I believe that this rock is her relationship with her partner.

♂ **His tip**

Isn't she doing an amazing job looking after your offspring? And she even tries to make time to listen to you when you come home from work. What she probably needs more of right now is time to herself. You can easily set this up for her by insisting that you prepare her a bath together with music, essential oils like lavender and chamomile, candles and rose petals. Put out some fresh, fluffy towels. It's most important that you take charge of the baby so that she can have this time to chill out without a sound in earshot.

♀♂ **Couple time**

Plan to have a lovely hot bubble bath together the next time you put baby to bed. Make sure you have plenty of hot water and lots of bubbles – the more bubbles, the more fun you will have together. Having bubbles in the bath means that you'll be able to be naked together in front of your partner without feeling that you're unveiling your post-natal body before you're ready to. Sitting face-to-face is ideal for chatting, while sitting between legs is ideal to give each other a head and shoulder massage. However you fit together in the tub, set out to have the most laughs and the best time you've had for weeks. Laughing together brings you closer and it may be one mood that you've been lacking recently amidst the other raw emotions.

Every woman needs a rock to lean on, particularly at times when she loses sight of who she is. You may have been capable and confident in your life before the birth and now you find yourself to be disorganised and forgetful. It's a big leap down from high-powered career to changing nappies and it can also feel like a long way to fall in the balance of power within your relationship. Remember it's only a phase and that you will get your strength back on all levels, even more than you had before. For now, it's normal to feel vulnerable as the mother of a new baby and to have a greater need for the protection of your partner through this time. He will be delighted if you allow him to help you through this time. Taking care of his pack is the male *raison d'être*. Reward him with what he may most desire – a little piece of you, preferably a physical piece. Shock, horror! I can hear you shouting at me already. Maybe you've slammed the book shut. How could I make such a suggestion? Well this is how it is. It's the reality and I'm going to say it now and I'll say it again throughout the book.

When I say 'get physical' I mean brush against each other as you pass by. Hold hands, cuddle and sit close to each other on the sofa. Before birth you would have probably not noticed the nourishment that these small gestures were giving to your sexual relationship and now they must become your staple diet. By being consistently physical with each other, you will start to feel more relaxed and confident that he isn't going to come on to you at any given moment.

WHEN CAN YOU HAVE SEX?

By now you'll both be wondering if this playing together will go any further. It's quite usual for an episode in the bath to lead into some slippery sex. For this reason, it's best to get these expectations and possible concerns on the table right away by talking about them *before* you get undressed. Please don't misinterpret this as me saying that it's too soon for you to be making love. There's no absolute rule about whether you can or can't have sex before your six-week check. Six weeks is a guideline and depends very much on how you feel, emotionally and physically, after the birth. Your midwife or obstetrician would prefer you to wait, to be sure everything has healed up well and that your uterus has returned to its normal size and position. If there is a medical reason why you shouldn't have sex before this time, then you will already be aware of this. Most of all, remember that it must always be the woman's choice to engage sexually and that she should never feel rushed into doing anything until she feels ready. If there's any pain or discomfort then wait until your check-up for reassurance.

Half of all mums tell me that they prefer to wait until after their six-week check to feel confident to resume sex. The other half prefer to try it for themselves first and then take any questions and concerns to their check.

It's a good idea to prepare for your six-week check with your doctor. If you are concerned that you may become flustered and forget your questions then write them down. You could even email them to the practice in advance of your appointment. Remember to mention any genital or breast soreness and any concerns you may have about resuming lovemaking. These might be emotional or physical or both. If you have any doubts, insist that you have a physical examination to reassure yourself. This is also a good time to talk about contraception, even if you don't think that you will need it at the moment. It's always best to be prepared. There is more information about contraception in Chapter 5.

It's important that you don't put pressure on yourselves. The good news is that most couples find themselves returning to regular lovemaking at some point within the first year. Performance pressure is a libido killer on its own, closely followed by desperate tiredness and physical exhaustion. These feelings are normal. It's how and what you do with this reality that will make the biggest impact on your sexual intimacy.

Don't be shocked if you do feel your libido surge for a while after birth. This seems to happen when your heart is opened wide at the sight of your newborn baby. It's the pure love that you're both feeling towards your precious baby. One mum described how there was so much love between them that she constantly felt like making love with her partner during the early days. They both enjoyed this feeling immensely and it helped to deepen their bond as parents and lovers. Many new parents find themselves together in a great pool of love and they are amazed how easily this intimacy can turn into sexual arousal. I've heard many stories of women who can't wait to get home from hospital and into the arms of their partners. One mum told me about her secret hospital blowjob with her husband. She felt so liberated that he had seen all of her wildness and vulnerability during birth that there was nothing left to expose. After all, sex can be sweaty, noisy and unflattering, just like giving birth. What a winning combination: pure open-hearted love and wild, primal passion. My advice is simple. If the desire is there and your body feels healed and up to it then go for it. Don't waste a moment of that precious energy and potential connection with your lover and the father of your child. Remember that being sexual doesn't have to include intercourse.

3

Month Two

Give yourselves a big pat on the back for getting through the first month of being a mum. This time couldn't have been harder on your body, emotions and potentially your relationship. Be kind to yourself, especially if you're feeling exhausted and bewildered about who you are or unhappy about your appearance. All is not lost; it's quite normal for new mums to feel like this throughout the early months, especially when you are on 24-hour call to your baby. What's not normal is expecting to be back to the woman or partner you were two months or a year ago.

This chapter is loaded with tips for both you and your partner on how to boost your intimacy without having to engage sexually. There's also advice on how to improve your own self-esteem as the new sexy mum that you are, by touching yourself with as much compassion as possible.

BREASTFEEDING

After the physical war wounds of childbirth, breastfeeding has the next biggest impact on your body. You can never underestimate just how much havoc it can play on you physically and emotionally through the early months. I am not suggesting here that you shouldn't feed your baby yourself, as I'm a strong supporter of breastfeeding. But I do feel that mums should know that they are not alone in their need to have a really good moan about how difficult and confusing breastfeeding can be. As complex as it must be for the body to make milk, it feels equally as complex to a mum's internal wiring. For example, it may change how you feel as a woman, throw you into confusion over your identity or force you to question whether breastfeeding can make you feel sexy. Even if you are not breastfeeding, you're bound to share many similar dilemmas with one another.

Many mums tell me that breastfeeding makes them feel as sexy as a lactating cow, with ginormous udders flip-flapping about. They do not like their breasts looking so big, floppy and veined; nor do they like the colour and size of their nipples.

I urge you to try to resist creating negative images about your body. Our thoughts are extremely powerful and often influence reality. It's tempting to be critical but try to think instead: 'My breasts are beautiful, if a little larger than normal. They're doing an amazing job and I'm happy that my body is working well.' See if you can spot the breastfeeding mum who feels comfortable with how her breasts look. She won't just dollop them out with a look of disdain. Watch the way she gently and sensitively touches herself and then copy her. Enjoy sensuously massaging your breast in the bath. This will also help to cut down your risks of developing mastitis by keeping the ducts and glands clear.

On the positive side, breastfeeding can be deeply satisfying for you on many levels. So much so that it's not unusual for mums to not want any other physical contact outside of this. Breastfeeding all day and night can push you to the point of physical saturation. You can't bear the idea of anyone making any further demands on you. All your cravings for physical intimacy can be met by looking into the eyes of one small bundle of love and joy.

I know that it's hard to hear but try to understand and recognise that your partner needs a little bit of physical contact time with you too. It could be in the form of a quick kiss and cuddle or briefly holding hands. He needs to feel that his place in your arms and heart hasn't been completely replaced by your baby, who spends most of the day and night there. If you can do it, then it will help to keep some spark between you.

Many breastfeeding mums find the idea of engaging sexually quite unappealing and even distasteful. This isn't surprising when you realise that you are flooding your body with the hormone oxytocin, also known as the happy hormone, whenever you feed your baby. This hormone is produced by the pituitary gland not only during breastfeeding but also during sex – it's the orgasm hormone. How lucky is that? There is such a thing as a free lunch after all and do you see now why you feel so full? Having literally hundreds of orgasms throughout the day, how would you ever be hungry for sex?

Look out for the women who find breastfeeding a real turn on, there may be more than you imagine out there. So are they more sensitive to the oxytocin rush than you or just not afraid of what people will think – to admit that breastfeeding turns them on? Talk about it with other mums and see if you can expose this well-kept secret that breastfeeding mums share levels of satisfaction with the multiorgasmic woman.

If you do find yourself feeling sexy and aroused with your partner, you may notice that your vagina feels quite dry compared to before birth. Don't panic. Your lubrication is affected by your hormonal ebbs and flows, as is any vaginal tenderness you may experience – unless you are still healing from the birth trauma.

Use plenty of water-based lubrication before you begin any sexual touching. See the resources section for product suggestions. Make sure you use generous amounts, applying it with your hands. Reassure your partner that what is happening to your body is quite natural and that your change in libido and lubrication is not because you no longer find him attractive. Go slowly and gently with everything that you do together. The more stressed you are, the more likely it is that your vagina will become dry and uncomfortable. If this happens, stop immediately and have a cuddle instead. Never force anything that hurts.

Have you noticed how your breasts start to leak the moment your partner touches you? Worse still, you may have already squirted him in the face. For some of you this will make you laugh and for others it will be too embarrassing for words. Not only do your breasts feel like they belong to someone else, they are now behaving like they do too. You may feel like wearing a large sign across your chest saying, 'Danger, do not touch.' But the bad news is that you only have to think of your baby for a nanosecond to set them off.

Wear your bra whenever you are in an intimate situation with you partner but not, I repeat NOT your grey washed-out feeding bra that is stuffed with breasts pads. This bra will not help you to feel sexy. Please buy yourself a couple of very sexy bras in a larger size. They don't have to fit you perfectly – in fact the more you have to stuff your breasts into the cups the better. They are your sexy 'dressing up' clothes to help to boost your self-esteem. Some mums also suggest wearing basques to keep their tummies pulled in too. If you have got some tatty-looking feeding bras I would suggest throw them away today and replace them with some pretty, properly fitted ones. It will lift your spirits to see your breasts in something that looks good and you'll feel almost like the normal you again.

Now that I've mentioned the old grey feeding bra I need to also bring up the topic of the big knickers. How did I know? Well, the simple answer is because every other new mum is wearing them too. It's important that you feel physically comfortable, especially with all the extra demands you currently have. It's also very impractical to wear a sanitary towel with a g-string. Nothing feels more uncomfortable than trying to squeeze your body into clothes or underwear that are too tight and force your bits to bulge out.

If you can't wear your sexy underwear in these early months, then why not get pleasure from looking at them? I suggest that you peg them out on the line (no need to wash them first) or put them on the drying horse alongside the baby grows. This will certainly keep you amused, especially if your partner imagines that you are wearing them every day. Meanwhile, you can still feel relaxed and comfortable in your granny's best with my blessing.

Better still, once you have stopped bleeding, take your underwear and your clothes off as much as possible at home. Many new mums tell me that they feel better naked than they do squeezed into their clothes. It's too easy to hide our bodies under layers of clothing especially if you have a baby during the winter. It may feel like you need a cocoon to protect you from the harsh reality of the outside world. Like the feelings of being judged for the way you look by other mums, who you perceive to be doing better than you.

These feelings are quite natural after you have had a baby. You will struggle with your body image, whether you are half a stone or three stone heavier than you were before your pregnancy. This is part of the great mystery and the confusion of becoming a mother or even of being a woman. You may need to appraise every part of yourself from the tip of your toes to the top of your head as you adjust to the new you.

Whenever you pass a mirror over the next few weeks, stop and look at yourself for a moment with your clothes on and off. If you find the idea of standing naked in front of the mirror confronting, then build up to it slowly. I suggest that you take small steps by first looking in the mirror at your head to your breasts, then from your breasts down to your pelvis, then from your hips to your feet. Each time you look, find something positive to say about your body. Yes, you will see saggy bits and bulging bits and stretch marks and scars, but it couldn't be any other way! These are your badges of honour for what you have been through. Be kind to yourself; your body has done a great job, you birthed a new life and deserve to be praised.

KEEP IT POSITIVE

We all like to hear positive things about ourselves and they can be particularly uplifting for us at times of personal weakness. I use this term 'weakness' advisedly, but I would generally describe this post-natal time in this way because I believe it is a period when we are literally weaker in our bodies after giving birth coupled with the demands of looking after a new baby. It's good to be able to admit this without feeling like a victim. However, over the years that I have been working with couples, I have noticed how little we remember to say positive things to each other. It's not like it was when you were first dating. It seems that once you and your partner become settled in the relationship and have children together, the compliments occur less and less.

We find it easy to be nice to the people we hardly know yet can be so cutting to our loved ones. It's a pattern of behaviour that I'd like to see parents breaking. In the long run, this will help to create a more harmonious family environment and a nicer world for our children to grow up in.

♀♂ **Couple tip**

Imagine that you are stroking each other with kindness and love when you say these positive things to your partner. Our bodies love to be touched in this way and soak up the attention. Add to the mix real touching and you will have the perfect intimate cocktail.

Lovers tip

Give each other as much positive feedback as possible, even if it is through gritted teeth at first. Be assured that you will soon find this second nature. Praise your partner for even the smallest positive thing that they do. It may seem patronising and you may feel silly but descriptive praise is a powerful and transformative force. One couple described this process as literally hosing each other down with descriptive praises.

Here are some examples:

'Even though you're really tired, it's good to see you smile.'

'I really appreciate that you gave me five minutes to read the newspaper when I came in from work.'

'Thanks for noticing I was really stressed and taking the baby from me.'

'I noticed that you made an effort not to talk to me when the baby was crying. Thanks.'

These statements are simple but highly effective. They only require you to find one positive aspect, no matter how small and insignificant. Even on the days when you are too tired to think straight, let alone have a conversation, this will keep your intimate connection alive. Remember the good old days when you thought everything he said and did was fantastic? I'm sure it felt very good. This is an easy way to rekindle these times. If you don't believe it's possible then try it and see.

THE POWER OF TOUCH

I strongly suggest that you put aside time each week to massage each other. Make it during the day on the weekend rather than late in the evening during the week when you are both exhausted. You will only need an hour but it is important to schedule and agree together when this will be. Write it on the family calendar to make it official. If you have a baby that doesn't sleep then please ask a friend to push your baby around the park so you can have this quality time together. It's always worthwhile saying why you need their help, as most people will be more willing if they know this.

I cannot emphasise this enough – you need to have time together every week without your baby to nurture your intimate relationship.

If the idea of getting physical with each other is sending you into a spin, then you wouldn't be alone. It's one of the most challenging aspects of becoming Mum and Dad together and it seems to be the one that has the most potential pitfalls for couples. Whether we like it or not, all of our pent-up

> ## ♀♂ Couple time
> Spend time discovering your erogenous zones of your body like the ears, eyes and feet. Unlock the pleasure by licking, kissing and sucking the lobes of each other's ears. Gently tickle the eyelids with your tongue. Rub the inner thigh with the sole of your well-oiled foot. Play with each other's feet, especially the toes. Caress each other's hands as you would like your own body to be caressed.
>
> Tell each other what you like when you are giving and receiving. Spend equal time in both roles as giver and receiver. Dim the lighting or shut the curtains but please do not do this in the dark as eye contact is essential if you are to deepen the intimacy between the two of you. If it's winter, put the heating up so that you don't get cold.

♀♂ **Couple tip**

Send each other something called a 'promise of favours cheque' before the session to tell your partner what you would like to offer them. It may say that you promise to give them an erotic foot massage. See the resources section for where you can get this chequebook or make it yourself on a postcard or piece of paper. See this as a good opportunity for doing something more sexual at a later date. This gives your partner the opportunity to decline what you are suggesting if it doesn't feel appropriate to them. Nobody should ever do anything that they don't feel comfortable with. In this way you are keeping the sexual fire between you both alight.

There is no obligation to be completely naked to massage each other. Your neck and shoulders are a good place to start as we all carry a lot of tension there, especially breastfeeding mums. Get into this weekly habit and don't put it off with excuses like you're too tired or the washing needs to be put away.

This way of intimate touching doesn't re-place sex but it will help you to stay physically connected. Giving each other a shoulder massage in front of the television is much better than not having any contact at all. See this time as a wonderful opportunity to discover new and sensual places on each other's body. In the routine of everyday life, most of us move quickly into having intercourse but I'm suggesting that you don't do this in these sessions. Instead, you begin to develop an erotic map of each other. The general rule is that the more vulnerable the body part, the more sensitive it will be to pleasure but I'll leave you to find that out for yourself. Each time you discover new and exciting places, you will be able to incorporate them into your future lovemaking sessions. This will expand your potential for pleasure together. Remember to touch the genitals last and build tension in the tease.

feelings of guilt, boredom, anger and despair will generally be reflected in our sex lives. It would have been like this before children too, only there are a lot more emotions around now that you have a baby together. Many couples feel justified in withholding sex and intimacy if they are angry or annoyed with each other but, in reality, it is ourselves that we are punishing the most.

We all need tenderness and a loving touch to survive on this planet. I know that many of you will argue with this, especially those of you who feel fulfilled by the sensual connection with your baby. Like many other new mums, you may see this post-natal time as a perfectly good reason to have a break from sex.

♂ **His tip**

You will find that her body feels and looks different from before she gave birth. It will probably be bigger and more voluptuous than when you first got together. Make sure that you tell her how great it feels to touch her.

A body that is bigger is also softer and this allows you to get into the texture of her curves. Give her lots of positive feedback about all the new and exciting places that you find on her body. She'd much rather hear about how she feels to you than how she looks, as she is probably ultra sensitive about her appearance right now. Even if you say that she looks great and you mean it, she may not believe you!

♀♂ **Couple tip**

To spice things up, I suggest that you play what I call the 'dice game' together, as this will leave where you touch each other to chance. Give parts of your body a number, for example, one is your shoulders, two is your head, three is your hands and four is your arms etc. Roll the dice and then massage and touch each other on the part of the body that corresponds with the number it lands on. You may want to roll a second dice to determine how and with what you touch each other. For example, one is licking, two is kissing, three is stroking etc. You could build up the excitement by preparing your dice numbers in one session and then waiting until the next available time to play the game together. Anticipation can be a real turn-on, especially when you are short of time.

If this is resonating with you and you gave birth just a few months ago, then you are on track with nature. You should be powerfully bonded with your new baby at this time and you'll probably be feeling that you are inside a magic bubble together. If however your child is over a year old, then it's worth considering how truthful you are being with yourself and your partner. Is it possible that your all-absorbing closeness with your infant is partly just a good excuse for not getting back to business with your partner? This question may come as a shock to you, but the one fact that we are not told, is that good parents have a sex life, and happy parents raise happy, healthy children.

If you are finding excuses not to be physical with your partner, then the best policy is truthfulness. Say how it is for you. If you feel stressed by the thought of any physical contact, then you really do need to tell him this, as he will be feeling you withdraw, which could create more unspoken confusion between you.

Many mums feel concerned that a simple massage will lead to more and that their partners will put pressure on them to engage sexually before they feel ready. Sometimes women feel that it is their duty to be sexual with their partners even if they do not want to. I strongly disagree with this. Our partners need to know that their sexual needs, wants and desires are not wrong but that they are theirs and not ours. He needs to take responsibility for them himself. Hopefully, in a different time and space, they will be most welcome.

If you do not feel ready to be physical with him then tell him why as nicely as you can. Make sure that he understands that you are rejecting physical intimacy rather than him. Explain your reasons, as far as you understand them. Ask him to listen to you and then to repeat back to you what you said. This will help you to be sure that he doesn't feel blamed by you for the situation. Let him have his say too.

ALL ABOUT DADS

Many mums tell me that dads need to accept that their contribution to the family during these early months is material rather than sexual. And as a mother, our natural role is to protect the baby at all costs. Don't neglect dad during this time and remember that he is also there to protect the child. I believe that these powerful but unspoken messages have the potential to cement his belief that he isn't useful or wanted any more around the family. It can be a common belief amongst dads that they aren't wanted when the baby arrives and these strong feelings can drive them away from home, as they don't feel welcome. One dad explained to me that men are not machines that you can turn off for this postnatal year and then switch back on when you need them again. This attitude and approach breeds resentment and can result in tension in the future.

Dads do not generally share their feelings with other dads. It's not the done thing. They seem just to get on with it, especially when it comes to being a provider for their new family. It's easy to hide away at work; it feels safer there, as it's a known territory, unlike the mysterious domestic kingdom back at home. It's no wonder that some dads dread going home at the end of the day, never knowing what level of chaos they will find behind the front door.

> ♂ **His tip**
>
> One divorced dad offered his wisdom by saying he wishes that he had been less selfish and less egotistical during these early months. In hindsight, he is able to see how much he has lost and wishes that he had realised that he was married to a whole picture that included the dog, the children and the tree in front of the house as well as his wife, who he saw as expendable. Most of all, he has realised that the early difficulties of parenthood are but a short time in their big lives as parents and it will pass.

From what I hear from dads, life with a new family can be like learning to juggle new balls. There can be so many pitfalls, especially at home, where trying to keep the peace can be like walking on eggshells. Take a look at these scenarios from fellow dads and see their solutions:

Scenario 1: He puts her six-week check with the obstetrician in his diary and rushes home from work that evening ready for action. She, on the other hand, feels stressed, rushed and finally extremely irritated. They don't have sex and still haven't.

Solution: Talk to her well in advance of the appointment about how you are feeling and how important it is for you to return to lovemaking. Respect her wishes and try to make a compromise around physical intimacy like massage that doesn't lead to sex.

Scenario 2: He tries to kiss and cuddle her when he comes home from work but she pushes him away with utter disgust. He feels like he has an infectious disease.

Solution: Tell her about how you feel when this happens, but not at the time it happens. Try not to blame her. She will want to be a good wife or girlfriend and greet you at the door but her physical capacity to give will be at its limit after taking care of the baby all day long. Accept that you are low on her list of priorities right now, but this will change.

Scenario 3: He finds the act of breastfeeding to be beautiful and natural. But although he loves to watch his child getting its needs met, he feels bereft that his partner's breasts are out of bounds to him.

Solution: Don't feel guilty if you feel a tad jealous of the baby's constant physical intimacy with your woman. If you can resist trying to push your way into her arms, she may allow you to discover new and exciting erogenous areas of her womanly softness.

Scenario 4: He tries to talk to her about his day and all the little annoying things that crossed his path whilst he was out of the house. She looks at him blankly; her ears are on standby for the impending baby cries. From within her world, she cannot hear him.

Solution: Book a babysitter and insist that you go out together, even if you just go around the corner to the local pub. Anywhere out of earshot of your baby.

The one common thread throughout these scenarios is the need to keep the lines of communication open between you both. Without this, you could get a sense of real helplessness.

♂ **His tip**

The world in which you find yourself currently is like a magical mystery tour for the average man and requires a good collection of survival strategies. The lack of sex during these early months may be the greatest hurdle for you, closely followed by tiredness. In your favour is the fact that lack of sleep can reduce your testosterone levels and lower your libido. However, this alone may not be enough to stop you twitching! If you are to remain monogamous through this time, then you will need to increase the time you spend in your own company.

Many couples never discuss whether or not they partake in the act of self-pleasuring or masturbation. It is something that one assumes and generally doesn't get discussed. However, this is your moment to lay your cards on the table about your secret pleasures. Let your partner know that this is your way of dealing with your sexual urges – you can do this on your own or invite them to join in. You can't make her responsible for your sexual satisfaction. Make it your mission to discover what gets you in the mood for sex. If you were in the habit of including mutual self-pleasuring into your lovemaking before you had your children, then the chances are that you will not find the potential to do it in front of your partner disturbing. Some dads I spoke to recounted moving scenes of them self-pleasuring whilst their post-natal partner snuggled alongside, sometimes feeding, sometimes not.

If on the other hand you prefer to be a private person about such matters, then the idea of doing this in front of each other may be too much to take on. Make small steps for now. Make sure that she is fully aware of what you are doing alone in the bedroom. Let her know that you are taking care of your sexual needs and taking responsibility for your sexual frustrations whilst there is little sexual contact with her during these early months. The main reason for such a level of disclosure is that it will help to reduce her guilt about not wanting or being willing to return to having sex with you. It takes the pressure off her if she knows that you are regularly taking care of your needs. This may free her up enough to want to get physically closer to you as she will not be afraid that your sexual urges (which are perfectly normal) will get the better of you. On a subtler note, you will put her mind to rest about why you are not super twitchy and stop her wondering if you are getting your needs met elsewhere.

Just for fun I have included the top-ten non-assisted self-pleasuring tips given to me by a veteran dad. This should keep you busy for a while. Remember that your sexual needs and desires are natural. Enjoy yourself and remember to share your pleasure around.

1. Make time because there is no rush towards ejaculation; remember that this doesn't have to be the only goal to spending sexy time alone with yourself.
2. Make sure that you will not be disturbed. Turn off the phone, tell your partner you are having 'you' time and turn off the baby monitor.
3. Set the scene for yourself by including candles, music and soft fabrics. Make it a place of comfort and relaxation.
4. To help increase your arousal you could dance in front of a mirror and wear your favourite clothes.
5. Pose and fantasise. Allow fantasy into your mind in whatever way.
6. Treat yourself to your favourite smells and food. Have a private picnic.
7. Go to a place that has juicy memories and relive them in your mind.
8. Look at erotic stories and videos.

9. Stroke your whole body, not just your genitals, with your hands, lips and fabrics.

10. Find your G spot and stimulate it, particularly as you are near orgasm. Your G spot is either between your scrotum and anus or it is inside your anus and is best reached with a pleasure toy. (See resources for more details.)

Giving plenty of time to yourself in this way is quite unusual for the average man but it will help you immensely if you are finding that your libido has lowered during your partner's pregnancy and following the birth. You will not be alone in feeling this way. Dads can be put off sex by seeing too much during birth, as you may have read in Chapter 2. You may also be feeling too tired with the demands of a heavy working day and no sleep to consider initiating or partaking in intimate delights with your partner or even yourself. You may also feel too pushed out and isolated from your partner to dare to engage with her sexually and for the fear of being rejected by her. All of these scenarios are quite normal. Total honesty, firstly with yourself and then with her will help you to regain your prowess.

If you find that your libido is ticking higher than his in these early months, count yourself lucky. Give him lots of opportunity to talk to you. The reason behind his lack of lustre may be very complex or quite straightforward. Right now you should put it out of your mind that it's about the way you look. Reassure him that you still love him and that there is still enough room for him in your heart even though you're a mum now.

♀♂ Couple time

Take the baby out in the baby carrier so that you can have a spare arm or hand for each other. Reach out and touch each other, pat each other on the bottom, slide your hand seductively down his/her spine. Really go for maximum contact with each other out on the street, within the bounds of the law of course. Help to raise the profile of new parents. And let people see that you are still a couple, not just parents whose only physical contact is fussing together over your baby.

The icing on the cake is to have a lovely long kiss together in the park. For this you will need to have your baby in the pram – unless you both have very long and flexible necks to wind around your baby's head in the sling.

We all know that couple love is very different from the kind of love that we have for our children. The intimate, sexual love that we share with our partners only has a place in the adult world. But what about all the cuddles, kisses, squeezes and hugs that we bestow upon our children? Yes, they deserve them because they're gorgeous and smell great. But have you ever considered how many times you kiss your child in the course of one day in comparison to how many you give to each other? It wouldn't take a rocket scientist to work out who's getting the most attention. Of course, it's an accepted fact that Mum and Dad will take turns to be physically glued to the baby but they are almost never glued to each other.

Have you ever considered that the people (I didn't say men) who designed pushchairs and prams clearly did not care about helping Mum and Dad to stay connected? Have you ever tried to hold hands whilst you push the pram? If you attempt this, please do it away from busy roads, ideally in the park. Many mums complain that this simply isn't possible. They feel that they are missing out on a fundamental part of their pre-baby relationship, the pleasure of strolling along and holding hands together.

THE ART OF KISSING

Why is it that we so often ignore the pure unadulterated pleasure of kissing? What I really mean here is having a really good snog – the kind of snog that gets your head swimming, your heart singing and your libido surging. Maybe you left all that behind with your teenage years, to concentrate on better, potentially more orgasmic things. There's no better time to rediscover how remarkably sensitive and responsive your mouths, lips and tongues can be, especially when they are up close to your partner's apparatus. It isn't only your genitals that have to be close to turn you on. Kissing stimulates the production of endorphins; these are the feel-good hormones and are a perfect pick-me-up during a tired lull. More good news is that the average French kiss burns about 12 calories. Not that that should be your only motivation. If you find that your partner has his mouth a little too wide to suit your taste then nibble the side of his mouth and he will automatically reduce the space.

♀♂ Couple time

For the sake of research, you could create your very own kissing laboratory! Increase the amount of times you kiss each other (not a peck), gradually over the course of several days. Also build up the length of time you actually kiss. Apparently, the average snog lasts around three and a half minutes. This isn't too long to leave the baby to coo and chumble alone, especially as it's for such a good cause! Remember to ask each other how you like to be kissed. Do you like French kissing with tongues? If so how deep do you like your partner's tongue to go inside your mouth? Do you like your lips gently nipped and nibbled? Do you prefer light, fluttery kisses or hard, passionate ones? How about moaning and groaning with pleasure? Licking and sucking each other's lips?

There are endless possibilities to suit all tastes. There is no reason why as parents you cannot find a couple of minutes to enjoy a great snog. If you do find yourself making excuses, then sit down together and have a serious chat in the ways suggested earlier in the chapter and find out what emotion is stopping you from wanting to kiss his/ her face off.

During feeding time you have a free hand so use it to develop your kissing repertoire. Your baby won't know if you check out different tongue techniques on the palm of your hand to find out what feels really exquisite. If you're breastfeeding then you'll have the added bonus of your body being pumped full of the oxytocin hormone, which will only increase your pleasure. Never a dull moment!

♂ His tip

There is a subtle nerve channel that connects her palate and upper lip to her clitoris, it's known as the wisdom conch-like nerve. Suck it and see what happens. This is a top ancient tip passed down over thousands of years from tantric rituals. Tell her that you have a similar one on your bottom lip.

4

Month Three

The subject of this chapter is your 'down there'. You may not believe that there is much to say about your vagina, but we can never have enough information about the workings of our genitalia. There's nothing to be embarrassed about; many of you gave birth through this place and it deserves this attention. Even if you think that you know everything there is to know about your vagina, I hope that you'll gain something extra here for yourself. It's not as simple as squeezing your pelvic floor muscles that gets you back into shape after the birth. Your genitalia contain a lot more than the muscles that hold your insides in and stop you from peeing yourself. They retain the memories and the emotions that you have experienced over your lifetime, all your sexual experiences, your gynaecological history and your birth stories. You may find this hard to believe but this could be the reason why women who have given birth ten years before, can still experience discomfort along their episiotomy scar whilst having inter-course, even though their doctors can find nothing visibly wrong. The vagina is essentially our personal place of power.

If you read this chapter before giving birth, I hope that some of the subjects will have stimulated your curiosity enough to write a list of questions to ask your doctors and midwives. You're not alone if your mind goes blank whenever your doctor asks if you have any questions. The same thing seems to happen to most of us when we are face to face with our doctors – many women tell me they feel disempowered at these appointments and that they retreat with their tail between their legs, more than often none the wiser. Of course this is an oversimplification and I do not mean to disrespect the medical profession in any way, but the truth is that the more you ask questions, the more you know, the more empowered you are, so it's best to start a list now and be organised.

I am presuming that you will open up this chapter not just before birth, but also randomly over the early months as your curiosity gets the better of you. In this way, like with the subsequent chapters, you may find that the information is useful to you before or after this month. Every one of you will have your own time frame on how and when you are ready to return to sex. It's a big leap for many mums to go from being a mother to a lover again. Perhaps by this third month you will be gaining confidence in your role as a mum. Try to take small steps now as you return to your role as a lover by relearning how to be a lover to yourself first. You must never be rushed into intimacy with your partner before you're ready but I'm giving you a gentle nudge here to kick-start your personal intimacy time. It's incredible how many excuses we can all make to avoid making time for ourselves. You are giving out physically, emotionally and sexually to the whole world but when it comes to giving a little to you, there's a high chance that you will fall straight to sleep instead. It's up to you to make time for yourself to gain the energy, confidence and pleasure that you deserve now and always as a mum.

Start immediately by taking a couple of long deep breaths, breathing in through your nose and filling your stomach and breathing out, long and slow through your mouth as if you are blowing down a straw. Relaxing, isn't it? This will hopefully make you realise how easy it is to chill out for a split second, even in the face of extreme chaos. By doing this quick and easy breathing, you may have become aware of how your body is reeling. You may have noticed that your heart was beating faster, that your normal breath was rapid and shallow and that you were not inhabiting any part of your body lower than your nipples. If you didn't get this awareness the first time, then take these breaths again and pay close attention to your body as you breathe in. Imagine that your intake of air is reaching all the parts of your body, right down to your pelvis.

Month Three

Many mothers describe a loss of sensation in and around their pelvis following birth. For some who have undergone traumatic experiences, the pain or fear of it can be so great that they cannot allow themselves to 'be' in this area for any longer than necessary. Even mothers who have had a gentle and easy birth can find reacquainting with their genitals a process they'd rather put off until tomorrow. It's sometimes easier to put the images of birth into the far reaches of our memories and when we focus on 'down there' it can bring them flooding back. It is through taking small and consistent steps that you will help yourself to heal any lingering traumas, whether they are physical scars and sores or emotional memories or fears.

The following advice is given in no particular order of importance. Nor is it written with the intention that you must have done all of it by the fourth month. Everything in this book and particularly in this chapter is an invitation. It's up to you to choose when and how you meet yourself 'down there' again. We all go at a different pace physically and emotionally and there is no one right or wrong way. Be gentle and kind to yourself and remember how brave you are to have even picked up this book and started reading it. You probably won't be surprised that many mums struggle with talking to anyone about their vagina, so you are not on your own if you do too. It's still not considered acceptable to give so much attention to this place. But in the context of birth and post-natal healing,

I'm hopeful that many of you will join me on the adventure. However, if you find that you have lots of strong emotions or flashbacks that don't ease when you talk them through with your partner or a close friend, it is important that you seek professional help. (See the resources section for more details.)

First of all, try looking at your genital area in the mirror and discover that your vagina is still a living, feeling part of you, despite what your mind may be telling you. If you managed to do this in late pregnancy, then you will hopefully feel easier about doing it now. It wouldn't be natural if you didn't still feel somewhat embarrassed or uncomfortable but I hope that your need and concern to see how you look following birth will spur you on. Find a time to do this when you know that your partner will be around to care for the baby. You need to know that you won't be disturbed so you can relax and not feel rushed. Before you begin, take several long and deep relaxing breaths, then prop yourself up against the wall or the headboard. You will need a hand mirror to look at your genitals and good light.

Time is a great healer and how long after giving birth that you look at yourself will obviously dictate what you see. Some women are so desperate to look that they do it within hours of birthing; others take a look before their six-week check and some would rather never look. The best news is that you will look much better than you think you do, whether it is hours, weeks or months later.

Be aware that if you have read ahead and are doing this within days of giving birth, your genitals will probably look swollen with oedema and bruised. The more gently you gave birth the less they will look like this and vice versa. If you have had stitches they will look enormous and ugly until they dissolve and as you will still be bleeding the area may be bloody. If you are used to using tampons then this alone can be a shocking sight to see. Best to take a bath just before doing this.

It's a good idea to have a genital anatomy picture at hand to help you to identify the different parts of your genital area (see the appendix). This is not a picture of an average post-natal woman, although it is not impossible for it to be this way. All genital appearance varies greatly from woman to woman, like facial appearance, so there is no need to worry if you find that you don't look exactly like the drawing.

Begin by looking at your pubic hair that covers the bone called the mons. Your pubic hair protects this sensitive area. If you had a Caesarean you will see the line of the incision above the hairline. Hopefully this is healing well.

Take your fingers gently down the centre of your outer lips to find the inner lips. These outer lips may completely cover the inner lips or the inner lips may hang down between the outer lips. Both variations are normal. If you are looking soon after birth, they will be swollen. Notice how the colour and size has changed since pregnancy. The colour will vary enormously between pink and brown but could be a shade of dark berries soon after birth.

The inner lips usually meet at the top of the clitoral shaft and here you will find your clitoris. The size of the clitoris and its distance from the vagina entrance varies from woman to woman. However most women find the clitoris is extremely sensitive to sexual stimulation and is the most important source of sexual pleasure. It is made of erectile tissue, hence it gets bigger when you are aroused and it has four times as many nerve endings as the penis. Yippee!

Now gently open your inner lips and look at the area around your vagina. Look at the shape of your vagina, its colour and design. Often it is compared to an orchid or other flower. As you look at it see if you can contract your pubococcygeus muscles (PC muscles) – there will be more on this later. Don't worry if you don't see any movement, it is still early days.

On either side of your vagina, to the north, you will see your urethra; this is where you urinate from. To the south, between your vagina and your anus you will see the perineum. This is the most likely place where you will see any stitches, tears or scars. Hopefully once your stitches are out, your scar will heal and fade away. However, notice if there is any inflammation or puckering and mention this to your medical carer.

Take your time doing this mirror exercise. It may be that you have several goes at it. Remember to breathe. This may sound obvious, but we often hold our breath, particularly if we are doing something new and different.

Try to think positive thoughts as you are doing this exercise, even if you don't feel completely comfortable with what you are doing or seeing. Many women, not just mothers, go through life without ever looking at their genitals. Nobody should force you to do something that you really don't want to do but remember that you will gain an increase in energy and vitality if you push through resistance. The sense of achievement you will get is always bigger and better than you imagine.

As you give more attention to your genital area, you are bound to become more concerned about how you look. It will go from necessity to priority. It's just like looking at yourself in the mirror and realising that you need your hair cut or coloured. It's quite possible that with the daily demands of the baby combined with your recovery from the birth, you haven't managed to have your regular wax and tidy up.

Ask your partner to give you a whole hour to yourself, preferably during the day. Collect your makeover kit together (see the resources section) and enjoy giving your genital area some really great attention and a little trim. See if you can give 'her' a whole new character to suit the new you.

YOUR PC MUSCLES

The sound of the words, 'Remember your pelvic floor girls', sends alarm bells and waves of panic running through most new mums. However, do not fear: it is never too late to tone and repair these vital muscles. In fact, it is better to give yourself a gentler time of it in the early weeks. It's almost impossible for you to feel the precise movements of the muscle after all that stretching during birth. It is vital to develop a routine that targets these muscles but it is just as vital to be able to feel recovered enough to be aware of what you are doing.

There are three areas to your pelvic floor, basically the front or urethral, the middle or the vaginal and the back or the anal. Each one needs toning as much as the other, especially to avoid any post-natal stress incontinence (urinary leaks when you cough or sneeze).

Only when you feel ready, perhaps towards the end of the first month, begin to squeeze the buttocks and lower abdominal muscles together as often as possible. Develop a trigger to remind you to do this. It could be something simple like every time you sit down to feed your baby, you do it 20 times or whenever you put the kettle on. Frequency is important and you will find that you begin to feel more as the days go by.

Then at around eight weeks, begin to pulse the urethral, vaginal and anal muscles individually for a count of three. It would go like this: pulse one, two, three, hold for a count of three then relax for a count of three. Do this three times for each area. An easy way to count this is to say two, two, three for the second set of squeezes and three, two, three for the third set. Again, remember to develop your own trigger to remind you.

The good news is that after a couple of months of doing these exercises, you will have outstanding muscles. It's like doing a gym work out for your genitals. Even bigger news is that the more toned your muscles are and the more control you have of them, the better sex will be. These muscles control the walls of the vagina and by regularly contracting them you will increase your potential for sexual excitement and stronger orgasms. There is more about this in the next chapter.

As you feel the muscles getting stronger, begin to squeeze all the areas together for a count of ten then release. Repeat this for five, increasing to ten times a go. Visualise bringing the walls of your vagina together. You may like to squeeze against, or even grip a specially designed 'toy' or your fingers to increase your strength (see resources). The larger the object, the more this will help you to increase your control during intercourse. Remember to relax fully after each set of squeezes.

It's important to be as relaxed as possible to help you to get the maximum energy gains from the time you spend focusing on your genitals. When we are stressed and let's face it, having sole responsibility for small people is super stressful, our muscles become tight and the many health benefits to deep muscle relaxation are limited. Taking the time to relax and visualise will help your body to heal and hopefully help you to sleep deeply whenever you get the opportunity. The visualisation transcript in the appendix will help you to reconnect to your genitals and to catalyse a deeper level of self-healing. It is best to record it with your own voice and play it through as you are lying down in a dimly lit room.

♂ His tip

Your love muscle is called the bulbocavernosus and this needs to be exercised just as much as hers, even though you haven't given birth. It's good for your health and good for your sex life. The way to find it is to cut off the flow mid-stream as you're having a pee. The muscle that you're using is your love muscle and you'll feel it behind your testicles, just in front of your anus. Aim to squeeze this muscle as often as you can, building up to 25 squeezes a go. It may help if you visualise pulling your testicles together.

Month Three

This process (and the others in this chapter) will have taken you to quite a deep level of introspection, which may have been uncomfortable at times. It's perfectly normal to feel like this, especially if it's the first time you've spent looking at your genitals. However, you can rest assured that for all the time you have given to doing these exercises, you will gain tenfold in energy. There's extra value in doing this after you've given birth as you have an opportunity here to bring any remaining trauma to the surface. You may wonder why you would ever want to do that. But think about it like this. You wouldn't want to walk around with a ginormous boil on your face, feeling like it's about to explode at any moment. This is how our unspoken emotions can feel if we don't find a way to express them. It can often help to get in touch with a deeper layer of your emotions by describing your genitals in words.

Go back and look at your genitals in the mirror and try describing what you are seeing rather than simply identifying the different parts. See what kind of images you have in your mind, your choice of words or any memories that surface. Do not worry if nothing comes to you. Try to remain relaxed and observe your breathing and your thoughts. Are you thinking about the shopping, the baby or the housework? All of this is quite normal. Maybe this is where your mind goes to during moments of physical intimacy with your partner? Do not beat yourself up. This exercise is to help you to get to know yourself better and to begin to listen to parts of your body that we so rarely listen to. It may help to try writing down your descriptions or even drawing what you're seeing. I am not going to give you a list of all the unpleasant and negative images I have heard from women when they describe their genitals, as this wouldn't serve you. But be assured that if this happens to you, you are not on your own. Sometimes it takes a while to see the positive images as you peel away layers of your past experiences.

♀♂ Couple time

You may want to share the process of rediscovering your genitals with your partner. You can do this by telling him what you have learnt; remember to stick with the positives. If you want to gain the most from doing this, you could show him your genitals whilst you talk. Remember, he's seen it all before. If he saw more than you'd have liked during the birth, this could help him to talk more about how he felt. The best position to do this is for you to rest back on to his chest, between his legs and position the mirror between your legs. He can then look over your shoulder into the mirror if you invite him to.

Month Three

> ## ♂ His tip
> Be aware of what a powerful and brave process your partner is currently engaging in. Let her know that you are available to listen to her. If she does want to talk or show you her vagina, try to remain calm and positive. Do not pull faces, look shocked or bored and do not correct what she says in any way. Recognise that it's your natural male instinct to try to make everything all right but don't follow through; if necessary, sit on your hands to remind yourself of this.

I recommend that you write down what you hear or even draw it. If necessary, try to create another image that is somewhat more positive. It may help you to throw out your original descriptions then rewrite them with a more positive stance.

Many women tell me how much they struggle with all of this, especially the idea of sharing this information with their partners. I can already hear you asking me, 'What's the point?' or being horrified at the thought and saying, 'No way!' Do you think that this bit of resistance may be telling you something? It's always hard for us to face up to feelings that we have about ourselves and our bodies and revealing this to our partner can be embarrassing and makes us feel weak. Remember that there's no rush and you don't have to deal with everything today – go at your own pace (or the baby's). What's important is that you feel good about yourself today. Then your appreciation of your genitals as a beautiful part of your body will happen in your sleep.

By now you may have looked and listened to this sacred part of your body but that still leaves the remaining senses of taste, touch and smell to explore down there.

Have you ever noticed how often you actually touch yourself? I'm not talking about touching yourself by coincidence, where you brush against your body as you're pulling your clothes on or as you're soaping up your body in the shower. Most of the time we don't even remember that we have a body, we're so locked into the habit of the action and we simply move too fast. So what I am talking about are the times when you touch yourself with tenderness just because you want to. You are probably wondering how would you ever have time for this, what with all the extra washing and daily chores and all that beautiful touching of your own baby to do.

Shut your eyes for a moment and take three lovely deep breaths. Imagine yourself swathed in the most divine, soft and luxurious fabric. Let it completely envelop you. Now see if you can allow yourself to feel the sensations of being touched by such softness on your body. Practice this over and over until you are able to conjure this image and the feeling at a click of a finger. It should take you no more than a few seconds. You can do it in the supermarket queue, while you are feeding or in your bed – the possibilities of where are endless. As are the many ways of being touched that you could cook up with your imagination. Try also being enveloped in hot sand or floating in warm, transparent water. I'm sure you will come up with lots of your own suggestions.

See this as the beginning of your training in fantasy. You may already be excellent at it, albeit a little rusty after giving birth or you may be a complete beginner. The type of fantasies that I'm referring to here are ones that can give you feelings of physical pleasure so it may take a little time to bring them alive. You can read much more about fantasies in Chapter 7 if you're already finding that your appetite is stimulated.

GENITAL TOUCH

Our bodies long to be touched and often we forget to listen to their callings for this. It's only when they are screaming out in pain that we eventually stop and notice. With mums, it will often be backache or shoulder ache from carrying or feeding. But have you felt any pain in your genitals recently? I hope that everything feels just fine down there. But whether there is pain or no pain, whether you had stitches or no tears and whether you delivered by Caesarean or vaginally, I would recommend that you do this touching exercise. This is an exercise that any woman can do at any stage of life but it is particularly beneficial after giving birth.

Whenever you touch your genital area with your own fingers with the intention of giving tenderness and love to this area, you will gain a lot. The power of touch cannot be underestimated; it soothes, calms, releases and most of all, it enables you to get to know who you are physically. The intention here is not to sexually excite yourself, although if this happens, then that's a bonus.

Find a comfortable place to sit — propped up on pillows on your bed is ideal. You'll feel best if you've just had a bath or shower, not only cleaner but more relaxed too.

Allow your legs to be comfortably apart. You can have a mirror between them or not, it's up to you. Take your time with this; there is no need to rush. Rather, you should try to linger a little.

Put a little lube onto two fingers and begin to touch the outside of your genitals. Allow your outer labia lips to stay closed as you sweep with gentle movements down towards your perineum (between your anus and vagina). There is no rush and your finger doesn't need to go inside your vagina.

Make small circles along your perineum, being careful to avoid touching your anus, as this will introduce bacteria.

Month Three

On another occasion, take time to massage around the anus, especially if you had third-degree tears that impacted here or have developed piles. Remember to wash your hands before you go on to touch your vagina.

Gently open the outer labia lips and take each of the small lips between your finger and thumb and roll them lightly. Remember to use plenty of lube as these lips are quite delicate. Everyone is different so you may feel inclined to pull and stretch them a little too. Just go with the flow.

Move up to the north side of your labia lips and locate your clitoris. It may be hidden in its hood or out and erect. However it looks, begin to circle around it. Allow your fingers to gently push into the fleshy area around it and discover how much of your clitoris is inside and how much is out. Keep in mind that everyone's anatomy is different and our body's reactions will change from day to day.

Take a moment to assess how you are feeling. Has your heart rate increased? Are you flushed or breathing faster? Have you stopped breathing altogether? Do you have thoughts and emotions distracting you?

If you need to take a break at this time then do it. You can always begin where you left off the next time.

If you're ready to continue then briefly rest your finger between your inner lips. How does this feel? It's unusual not to go straight on into your vagina isn't it? When you feel ready, gently move your finger into the inside of your vagina, no more than up to your knuckle. Take a moment to breathe again. See if you can feel your pelvic floor muscles as you squeeze them around your finger. Remember that these muscles will regain their pre-pregnancy tone each time that you do this.

Try to rotate your finger around this inner part of your vagina and gently make tiny swirls with the soft pads of your finger. You can go either clockwise or anticlockwise. See if you are self-lubricating as you do this. If you feel at all dry then add some more lube to your finger.

From this place you will move into the inside of your vagina. You can spend as long as you have inside your vagina touching the inside walls with small circular movements. Try to move at 15-20 second intervals.

Pay attention to how you feel while you are doing this. It will be a new experience and you may be surprised at the variety of sensations you will experience here. This is particularly interesting as we are often led to believe that the only part of the vagina that has sensations is the first inch inside and the G spot.

See if you can find your G spot by hooking your finger behind your pubic bone. It will feel spongy and pleasurable.

Spend time massaging with slow, circular movements over any scar tissue from the birth. Do you experience any pain or unusual sensations here, like burning or tingling or sharp pains?

Whenever you find an area is painful or even dull, keep your finger on the spot and pulsate it. Notice the sensations and see how they change. Observe your emotions.

Most women are surprised how vast the space seems to be inside their vagina. The most common description is of it being like a cave. I like to think of it as an Aladdin's cave, full of jewels.

As you gently withdraw your finger from inside your vagina, take a moment to look at it. This may be a new experience for you but I cannot underestimate how important it is for you to know what your fluids look like. They will tell you a lot about your general health and where you are in your hormone cycle. I suggest that you look, smell and taste them. This will immediately alert you to any infection that may be lurking inside you (it will smell bad) and this will speed you along to getting treatment that you may need. If you are still bleeding after birth or if you have returned to monthly bleeding, then you may prefer not to taste your fluids but smelling them is still vital. Be brave; you will gain a lot from this.

I recommend that you try to repeat this at least once a month for the first year after giving birth and then every three months. It will also help you to reconnect to your natural bleeding cycle. It's possible that you may start your periods again even whilst you are breastfeeding and usually within several months of giving up. I have included in the resources section some nutritional and emotional suggestions to help you to regain your balance. Most mums feel more 'normal' once they begin to bleed again.

If you were suffering from either dyspareunia (pain on intercourse) or vaginismus (spasms of the vaginal muscles) then this process would be very valid for you too. Take your time with it. There is no rush.

You may have found touching your genitals arousing and naturally slipped into sensations of pleasure. This is great. Go for it. Never resist an orgasm.

If you haven't ever pleasured yourself to orgasm with or without using a sex toy, then I would suggest adding the following additions into the basic practice of what you just did.

You will all be very different, not just in how you look, but in your preferences to pressure and sensitivity. You need to experiment with different styles to find out what you want. You may also find that what you like one day has changed the next. Be aware also that the average woman can take 20 to 30 minutes to reach orgasm. Give yourself the best opportunity by getting down to this the moment you put your baby down for a nap – don't waste a second.

Touch your whole body with gentle, light touches. Include your stomach, breasts, thighs, neck and shoulders and especially your face, lips and mouth.

As you stroke over the vulva and squeeze and slide off the

edge of each of the lips, remember to breath deeply and to stroke up to include the breasts and nipples.

Increase the time you touch your clitoris. Circling it in one direction and then in the other. Stroke very slowly up through the inner lips and over the clitoris.

Return to massaging the inner thighs, buttocks and sweep down your legs.

You may want to stay with firm pressure and strokes around your clitoris, especially if you can feel yourself getting aroused.

As you gently introduce your finger, begin to massage the inner opening of your vagina, be sure to squeeze your pelvic floor muscles up to ten times. If you cannot feel anything at first, do not worry, this will change the more you practise.

When you feel that your vagina is in a relaxed state, softer and moister, then you are ready to put your finger further inside.

Extend your fingers up the front vaginal wall beyond the pubic bone until you touch the G spot. The whole of this area has the potential for pleasure. Vary the pressure, rhythm, fast, slow, vibrating and introduce a 'come here' movement with your finger over this area.

Combine this with stimulating your clitoris and breasts at the same time. As you feel yourself getting more and more turned on try to relax all the muscles in your body, breathe in and out rhythmically and allow yourself to make as much noise as you want to — this should tip you over the edge into orgasm.

♀♂ **Couple time**

Try and do this touching exercise together. The intention is not for this to become a lovemaking session. Rather, it is for him to learn to look after your genital area with love and tenderness and to not have expectations of his actions being reciprocated. You can't get better than this, especially after you have given out so much during pregnancy and particularly from this area during birth. It will be a whole new approach to genital contact together and for this reason it may be better to take your time rather than jumping straight in. This will also depend on your sexual history together and what you are both comfortable with.

Begin by showing him how to do it. You can lean back on his chest for support, your bottom between his legs and a mirror between your legs so he can watch you without staring right at you like a doctor. When you feel relaxed about him being there you can ask him to put his hand on yours as you touch yourself. This will help him to understand about the speed and rhythm to touch you with.

Whenever you do this together, take time to talk about what you have learnt, liked, didn't like and what feelings it may have brought to the surface for you both. Slowly move to him pleasuring you by himself.

You are very brave if you have even attempted to do this touching on your own, extra brave if you have done it with you partner and mega brave if you are able to allow him to do this for you. The most powerful ways to approach this are to not snap his head off if he forgets what to do or touches you too hard, to listen to him but not chat to him and remember to breathe to relax your body, as this will support you both.

I hope that you will revisit these little exercises from time to time in your journey through motherhood. They are very useful particularly during the many physical changes we have throughout our lives. Let them be there as a support and challenge for you to gain a deeper understanding of who you are as a woman and mother.

♂ His tip

This is not foreplay. Instead, it is an exercise which hopefully, in time, will lead to better intimacy and sexual connection between the two of you. You are giving your love and support to your partner to help her to recover from childbirth and no matter how easy the birth may or may not have looked to you, every one of your gentle touches will bring back energy and vitality to this area. Her genitals will release trauma and pain and become alive in your very hands. I know it will stretch you to not get turned on. I can only recommend that you have a really good self-pleasuring session beforehand to relieve tension and enable you to relax. The more you relax, the more she will too.

5

Month Four

You may be beginning to wonder if you will ever read about sex in these pages, especially as the word 'sex' is in the title. It's completely natural. What's not natural is our unwillingness to talk about it together in an honest and open way. We generally prefer to change the subject whenever the word sex crops up in conversation, especially now the baby has been born. But that's not so surprising when one of your so-called friends tells you how they were at it like rabbits a week after she gave birth or one the mums at the post-natal class shakes her head with disapproval when you say that you still don't fancy it. These people are exactly the reason why we don't discuss our feelings of sexual inadequacy. It is so disempowering. Believe me, we all have questions, doubts and fears about sex and issues of self esteem in the bedroom, particularly after having a baby. What you need right now is a special friend who's willing to listen to you throughout this time. Preferably, it will be someone who has a shared experience.

So to put your mind at rest, this chapter will include sex ... lots of sex. Sex as you may never have known it before. Sex for new or second- or third-time parents. Sex for one or sex for two. Sex for fun and sex for pleasure and sex to bond you as lovers, rather than just good friends. I use the actual word 'sex' a lot during this chapter in the hope that by the end, you will find it all quite normal. Just like not wanting sex for many months after childbirth is quite normal. Did you know that it takes most couples up to a year to get back to where they were sexually before they had children? Even if they were the couple that had already had sex in the first month. There's a multitude of reasons why this might happen and you will probably have many of the answers yourself.

The non-stop physical demands of parenting has to be top of the list of what is stopping you from having regular sex and I'll be offering you many suggestions to get around this from now on. But what motivates us to get back into it in the first place? My theory is that we are too quick to rush back into the sexual habits that we had before we had our children, rather than trying to find new ways of being intimate together. Ways that are more compatible with our lifestyle as parents. Sorry guys, but it's dads in particular who want to get things back to how they were before the baby, and who can blame you? Mums, on the other hand, have a multitude of reasons that motivate them to getting back into sex, such as:

'I feel guilty that I don't really want to but I should.'

'I feel bad that I'm not giving him any attention.'

'I feel that it's my duty – what else am I contributing?'

'I need to find out if it's all working down there.'

'I should keep up with my friends and with what I read in magazines.'

'I'm trying to get back to how it was before.'

'It will help me to find out if I'm still a woman, not just a mother.'

'I'm doing it to make sure that I keep my man.'

'I need intimacy and closeness.'

'I'm feeling so horny that I can't keep my hands off him.'

Are there any surprises here? There's nothing bad about having these feelings, it's simply good to recognise what motivates us to be sexual. However these alone are not sustainable in the long-term and may explain why we often run out of steam sexually, so to speak, within a few months of starting up again.

Take a moment to remember how your body felt when you first had sex in these early months: Did you feel aroused? Did you lubricate naturally? Did you have an orgasm? Did you experience any pain, tenderness or soreness in your vagina? Did you enjoy doing it?

If you haven't had sex yet, then you'll be able to ask yourself the above questions once you do. If your answers were a combination of yeses and nos then you're not on your own. Most new mums have difficulty relaxing enough to really enjoy sex in the early months. Even if you've been successful at getting your baby to sleep you will be feeling on edge that he or she may wake up at any moment. You may also be tense, particularly in your pelvis, as you'll be anticipating feeling potential pain in your vagina. It's also possible that you will feel uncomfortable with your body image in front of your partner. I reassure you that all of these feelings are natural.

What doesn't come so naturally to us is being able to change our habits, particularly our sexual ones. By this, I am referring to what we consider sex to be. Do we think of sex as just intercourse or could it be hand pleasuring and oral sex or even stroking each other all over with erotic intent? On a practical level all of these can be arousing enough to reach orgasm but only intercourse requires you to take contraception. Incidentally, this is another reason why women frequently avoid having sex in the early months – the fear of falling pregnant so quickly after birth is the biggest passion killer of all.

Let's get practical with some information that I hope will help you to navigate your way, safely and with greater pleasure through these months.

CONTRACEPTION

It's better to be safe than sorry with regard to taking precautions. I want to quash two myths outright. The first is that, if you are breastfeeding, you will not fall pregnant. This is not true, just look at all the second-time mums still breastfeeding their first through the pregnancy and ask them how come they got pregnant. The second is that it is safe to practice the withdrawal method. This is known as the Costa Rica method within the family planning world because there is enough sperm in the average man's pre-ejaculate to fertilise the female population of Costa Rica. Now, did that stop you in your tracks?

If you are still breastfeeding, the best and safest method is to use condoms. They are also useful to have on hand in case either of you get thrush, as they will stop you passing it back and forth. There are so many shapes, sizes and flavours of condoms these days to choose from. You can even put them into your supermarket trolley without feeling embarrassed. You could also have a Mirena Intrauterine System (IUS) fitted. This is a coil that is fitted into your womb through the cervix by your GP or obstetrician, within a week of beginning a period, and slowly releases progesterone. Alternatively you could take the progesterone-only pill. If you have a diaphragm from before your pregnancy be aware that they require good internal muscle tone to stay in place and need to be checked for size each time you increase or decrease in weight. See the resources for further suggestions for after breastfeeding.

 Lovers tip

If you are struggling with using condoms after all this time, I suggest that you have a condom play session together to boost your confidence. What counts is for you both to be able to roll them on to his erect penis with your mouth or by hand, with as little delay and fuss as possible.

First of all, squeeze the air out. It should be an exciting part of your foreplay, not something that turns you off. Buy yourselves a bumper pack and practise putting them on and off your partner from different positions and angles. Put a little lube into the end of the condom – this will not only increase sensitivity for him but will also help to reduce soreness. Have lots of fun doing this – nobody is giving you a score. If he loses his erection, try not to get stressed, just relax and start to rebuild the sexual tension again.

Month Four

AROUSAL CYCLE

Did you know that it takes the average woman considerably longer to get aroused than it takes the average man? It could take minutes for him to become fully aroused and ready to pop whereas it could be anything from 15 to 45 minutes for her to catch up to his level of excitement. This means that you will potentially need 30 minutes to really feel satisfied when you make love. This may seem like an impossibly long time but I'll be giving you tips that will help you to cheat a little with this in the following chapters. We all have four phases in our sexual response cycle: the excitement phase, the plateau phase, the orgasmic phase and the resolution phase. It's very empowering for you to have a little knowledge about these phases and their effect on your physiology. Try not to get too hung-up about them, though, especially if you find that your body isn't performing in this way. Give yourself a break and remember that your post-natal body is currently under siege by a complex web of hormones.

Take your mind back to the last time that you were both aroused. See if you can remember seeing any signs of this in each other. Did you notice that your breathing became more rapid? Do you recall getting a red flush on your chest or did your nipples increase in size and become erect or even sprayed milk? What you may have not noticed, in the heat of the moment, were the changes that were going on inside your vagina as you became excited. Let's look at what happens here through each phase and acknowledge why these phases are so beneficial for your post-natal body.

Within the first 10 to 20 seconds of becoming excited, your vagina will begin to lubricate. As you move into the plateau phase your lubrication will increase again.

You need lots of lubrication, especially when you first return to intercourse as this will help to reduce friction. Remember that your post-natal hormones can interfere with your body's ability to lubricate naturally. Also if you are at all dehydrated, this will have an effect on how well you lubricate. My advice is to use lots of lube – there are several brands available from your local chemist and you can even pick it up from the supermarket. You'll be surprised how this will increase your relaxation and your natural lubrication will flow even more, as if by magic. Also, remember to keep up your fluid intake, especially if you are breastfeeding, as this has a tendency to dehydrate you and dry out your vagina.

For each moment that your arousal builds in your body, so your vagina expands, lengthens and softens. With the knowledge that this space is increasing inside your vagina, you will be able to relax and worry less about your return to sex being painful.

Blood flow increases to the clitoris so that it gets bigger and harder and protrudes through the labia lips. This gives you and your partner easy access to a pleasure spot on your body. It's non-invasive but has the potential to increase your arousal rapidly. It's also the most common type of orgasm.

Your inner and outer lips puff and soften up with the extra blood flow and increase in size as you approach the plateau phase. They also change in colour to a lush deep berry red. You may recognise that you have arrived in this phase by your increased desire to be penetrated. That's if your brain is still working.

This engorgement of your labia and vaginal entrance helps to cushion any scar tissue from the birth. The whole area feels as if it has a velvety padding, which is quite liberating if you have previously felt tight. Use your mind to visualise this area full of luxurious velvet. Notice how this encourages you to relax, open up naturally and become more receptive to receiving your partner.

♂ **His tip**

You'll know that you've reached the plateau phase because your penis will be fully erect and you'll be raring to go. This is time for you to kick back a little and relax. See if you can connect with your potential for full body pleasure by trying to integrate other erotic parts of your body and reduce the focus on your genitals. This will help you to maintain your sexual tension without rocketing into orgasm and allow her to catch up with you. It could be anywhere between several minutes to half an hour. Long and slow breathing will also help, as does gently tugging down on your balls or squeezing your penis with two fingers, just below the glans.

Keep in mind that nearly all men experience problems at some stage in their lives with erections or either premature or delayed ejaculation. Stop worrying and look in the resources section if you need more information.

THE ORGASM

Having an orgasm is high up on most people's wants, needs and desires list and new parents are no exception to this. So how do you know that it's happening to you? Relaxation is key, especially for her.

It's a stress buster, good for your health and immune system, good for your skin, makes you more youthful, creative and is great for muscle tone. The most common reason that she won't have an orgasm is because of poor or non-existent foreplay technique and lack of time.

If you've never had an orgasm then the good news is that

there are many resources available to help you to do so today, ranging from information on the internet to books and even DVDs. The main suggestion I have would be for you to find your own place of pleasure through masturbation. If you don't know where your trigger point is then you won't be able to show him. Most women climax through stimulation of the clitoris, some through G spot pleasuring and less than 30 per cent of women have orgasms during intercourse.

♀♂ **Couple tip**

Here are the ingredients that you may need for you both to have an orgasm – relaxation, comfort, intimacy and heart connection, time and space, good techniques, an open mind, imagination, patience and a great sense of humour.

Let me begin by addressing your concerns and complaints in the face of this information:

'How are we ever going to have enough time to get through these phases?'

Sex is all about time management when you have a baby. This means that you will need to plan for your lovemaking sessions. They don't need to be hours long but they do need to be long enough to include a little taste of those magical ingredients. Choose times when you are least likely to be interrupted, for example don't rely on your baby's short nap time as you can be sure he won't shut his eyes for a moment. It's better to organise a babysitter so that you two can really focus on getting to know each other again. If your baby is good night-time sleeper, take advantage of every moment of this. Get together as soon as the baby nods off.

'We're always too tired to do more than think about sex.'

Change your habits. Sex at bedtime should be banned. You will never get the quality of sex that you deserve if you try for it with your eyes half-closed. Wake up earlier in the mornings (that's before your baby), or wake up together after night-time feed, or build it into your days off and weekends. Planning this together in advance will help to get you in the mood. You'll gain intimacy just by talking about having sex; it's a verbal foreplay or text foreplay.

'What happens if she doesn't catch me up before I come?'

First of all, let's drop the guilt if you come and she doesn't. Balance this out by making your next sex session a time when just she comes. You don't always have to ejaculate.

Month Four

Remember to use all your available tools to pleasure her – that's your mouth, hands, feet, and full body – and there'll be no reason why she won't catch you up.

'We can't possibly have sex as our baby is still sleeping in our room.'

Choosing the right time to put your baby into his or her own room is your decision and nobody should tell you what to do. I will tell you though that having your baby in the same room when you have sex doesn't work long-term. You will both feel uncomfortable and rightly so, as your sex life is your private affair. The solution is to change where you do it. If you have a spare bedroom, try there if you're looking for comfort or in the living room, kitchen or garden if you're looking for variety.

If you haven't convinced your partner to read any of this book yet then pull out the stops for this chapter. Offer him something he'd like in exchange for taking time out to read it. My suggestion would be a blowjob. This will get his attention.

Sex is about engaging with each other physically, verbally, through cyberspace or thin air in such a way that makes you feel bigger, better and brighter from the experience. Yes, you can get this by doing other things but the explosive quality that you get from getting down deep and dirty together is missing. You can always tell people who are sexually satisfied by the way they look. Yes, even post-natal ones. Their eyes are shining, their skin glows, their body moves well and you feel drawn to be near to them. Good sex is the best elixir for youth and vitality, better than any expensive face cream.

♀♂ Couple time

Have you ever talked to each other about what sex means to you? Or what it means to your relationship? Have you ever shared with each other what motivates you or what puts you off? This is a million dollar conversation. Just like sex, you need to plan for this, as it's not really a suitable conversation to have in the supermarket. Even if you think you know all the answers about your partner, remember that your priorities and ideas may have changed now that you are parents. Open up your mind to new suggestions.

If either of you said that sex doesn't have to include intercourse then you get a big tick from me. It can't be the only way or we would be so bored that we just wouldn't bother. Especially as the majority of women have orgasms through manual stimulation and oral sex, which doesn't require intercourse.

Month Four

Talking to each other is the best aphrodisiac on the planet. It is foreplay, especially if it has been a while since you spent any quality time together. How can you expect your bodies to know what to do together, if your hearts aren't aligned first? Having children together, as we've seen in previous chapters, is a sure way to fall out of alignment with each other. Combine this with sleep deprivation and physical exhaustion and it's surprising that our children ever have siblings! Believe me, a good number of your fellow mothers would rather go out with girlfriends for a good chat, than have sex with their partners. So this tells us how important talking, or rather being listened to, is for women.

♂ His tip

I am certain that you haven't got this far in life without realising that men and women are different. You get turned on in life by fixing things, whereas women like to talk things over (please excuse this oversimplification). What I am saying is that you need to talk to her before you try anything remotely sexual. Actually, you don't even need to talk. What matters is that you listen to her talk about how she feels. Grab the chance to do this whenever you see an opportunity and gain some points.

The New Mum's Guide to Sex

A woman will generally need to communicate with her heart, before she is up for sex versus a man will go for sex first then be ready to speak what is in his heart.

Most veteran parents tell me that one of the most successful things that they ever did was to make a regular weekly commitment to spending an evening out together. This means that you book a babysitter for the same night each week. You then go out for dinner together or to the pub or to a café or to the park or anywhere that is out of the house. It's too easy to make excuses not to do this – the best one is that you can't afford a babysitter. If this is true, then I suggest that you set up an exchange with other new mums. The second excuse is that dad can't always get home early enough or guarantee that he will have the same night free each week. I put my foot down to this one; he needs to put it into his diary. If he can get to a daytime business meeting then he can get to a restaurant for an evening date with his beautiful partner. He needs to challenge his motivation here. If you are going to meet at the venue, then book the babysitter to come to help you do the bath and bedtime routine. This should give you time to have a bath, style your hair, fix your make-up and choose your outfit. Pampering yourself is important, as this is part of the pleasure. One mum told me that even if her partner couldn't make their evening appointment, she would still keep the babysitter and go out with her friends.

Month Four

I wish you good luck talking to each other. The advantage of going out regularly is that you can't possibly only talk about your baby week after week. No offence intended but you will be forced to expand your conversation beyond what it would be if you were at home together.

So if you believed my male and female model of sexual communication about heart-to-sex and sex-to-heart, then you will be expecting to have lots of sex after your date night. I'll give it to you straight: don't get your hopes up too high as you'll probably be exhausted by the time you get home. Please try to resist the temptation to give up your night out together because you're not ripping each other's clothes off the moment the babysitter goes home. This may happen once or twice out of every ten dates. Whenever it does happen, celebrate and savour every moment.

See the other eight dates as foreplay for a future sexual encounter. You need to be realistic through these early months. It's unlikely that you will have the time, energy or inclination to have a seven-course sexual banquet just now. What I am suggesting instead is that you sample a course at a time of equally delicious food. Each one has the potential to satisfy you and they naturally lead you to the next course.

You probably did this when you first met unless the earth moved the mountains and you had all seven courses at once. Most of us start out by dating, which means you talked and got to know each other first to develop your intimacy with one another. We then move to kissing and petting, then to hand and oral pleasuring and then to the big sex thing. Have you ever felt disappointed that this last course wasn't as good or as satisfying as you had dreamed that it would be?

Unfortunately it often happens this way. Intercourse isn't always the bee's knees that we all make it out to be. Especially as so few women can orgasm through this alone. I'll introduce a few tips later in the chapter to help to remedy this.

 Lovers tip

Never take it for granted that you know what your partner wants and desires sexually, especially after giving birth. You are responsible for telling each other how and where you like to be touched, kissed or licked. Sometimes it's easier to hurt each other with harsh criticisms and complaints, rather than to empower each other with constructive suggestions.

Help each other by showing and telling one another how you like to be touched with your hands. Ask your partner to put a hand on top of yours and follow your lead. When they go it alone, give plenty of feedback to encourage them. This could be with noises of appreciation rather than words.

Month Four

Even though you now know that sex doesn't equal intercourse, it can be easy to forget and fall into bad habits. Luckily, this post-natal period is an excellent time to make new habits, in how you approach your lovemaking now you are parents. Here are seven habits to live by:

1. You will go on regular dates together.
2. You will kiss and hold hands frequently and for longer.
3. You will listen to each other's feedback about what you like and dislike.
4. You will touch each other without diving in.
5. You will give excellent hand pleasure to each other.
6. You will give outstanding oral pleasure to each other.
7. You will know when and how to introduce intercourse.

If you haven't self-pleasured before or since you've had the baby, then go back to the previous chapter for some hints. Take your time; it's vital that you feel relaxed. I would also recommend that you try out a couple of the fantasy suggestions that are listed in the resources section. You will discover whether you are most turned on by listening, reading or watching fantasies. Remember to tell your partner which one gets you going the most.

Nobody likes to admit they are lacking skills, particularly when it comes to pleasuring each other with their

♥ Lovers tip

Being skilled in pleasuring each other with your hands is invaluable as you don't have to take your clothes off, you can do it in the car or under the restaurant table, you can bring him to orgasm even if you don't want to join in and whilst you are healing internally or bleeding, you can still enjoy clitoral orgasms. For less direct genital contact, you can stimulate the internal clitoris by pressing into the pubic hair just below the pubic bone.

hands or mouth. Yet it's natural that you would be a little naïve, especially if you haven't given these lots of consideration in your relationship before. It's not a great idea to blame this on other things, like not having enough time because of the baby. Try to tell the truth, at least to each other.

HAND PLEASURING

These dos and don'ts of hand-pleasuring are your staple ingredients. It's up to you to develop your own menu, to suit your personal tastes. Remember to have a few laughs as you learn – especially if you are all fingers and thumbs.

♂ **His tip**

Touch her half as hard and at half the speed that you touch yourself. Remember to include her whole body, not just her genitals.

An easy way to develop your lighter touch is to practise touching a flower head, one that reminds you of her. Notice how softly you need to touch the petals, then, touch her like this. She will really appreciate this after childbirth. But be ready to increase stimulation at any given moment. Women can suddenly want a much firmer touch, especially when they are about to orgasm. Listen for your instructions and read what her body language is telling you.

DON'T turn off the lights.

DO set the scene with candles, aromatherapy and music.

DO start off slow and speed up as he goes towards orgasm. Touch his whole body.

DON'T be too gentle or too hard, you really could hurt him and turn him off.

♂ His tip

DO use lots of lubrication. Saliva and pre-ejaculate are not always slippery enough. Warm it in your hands before you put it on for each other with sensuous strokes over the whole area. Reapply it throughout to keep her wet.

DON'T sit between her legs as this may take her back to the memory of giving birth.

DO get into a comfortable position. Dad, you could be there for at least 20 minutes. Try lying beside her, reclining back on some pillows.

DO massage her inner thighs and cup the whole of her genital area in your hand, applying a circular movement. Stroke and tease her body.

DON'T dive straight in.

DO wait until she invites you to go in deeper. Be alert and aware as she may speak with her body language not words. The best clue is when she opens her legs wide.

DON'T push your fingers inside her vagina until she is aroused. Again, look for the signs or ask her.

DO stroke and squeeze the outer and inner labia lips and roll the clit between them.

DON'T directly stimulate the clitoris but tease and circle it in different directions.

DO vary your pressure and rhythm. She will guide you with her pelvic grinding.

DON'T be put off if she doesn't seem to be getting aroused, it can creep up on you.

DO make a 'come here' movement across her G spot. (To locate it, see Month Three on page 111.)

DON'T poke around in her vagina or rub any scar tissue.

DO combine clitoral with G spot stimulation and remember to touch her whole body.

DON'T change techniques or speed if you feel her heading for orgasm. Keep at it.

DO begin to stimulate another part of her body the moment she has reached orgasm.

ORAL SEX

Did you feel yourself hunger for a little oral when you were pleasuring each other with your hands? It does feel that one naturally slips into the other, if you'll pardon the pun. But like all techniques, this doesn't have to be the way. Licking, kissing and sucking one another down there can happen just because you fancy it. You don't need a goal, simply relax and let this be an aperitif for something else later. Sex shouldn't be a once weekly or monthly explosion. Adopt a 'little and often' approach. You can weave this much more easily into your family life. It also keeps you on your toes, looking for opportunities to enjoy yourselves.

The number-one rule is that you are clean, trimmed and well shaven. Be aware that stubble, whether it's up top or down below, could give your partner a nasty rash.

Oral sex is an excellent way to be intimate together after you've had a baby because you won't get pregnant again doing it. It's also gentle on the female genitalia if you are still healing from birth and you can choose a position, like straddling his face, in which you can stay in control of the pressure.

You can show him how you would like him to use his tongue by demonstrating on the flat of his hand.

♀♂ **Couple tip**

DO concentrate on what you are doing — looking around the room is a turn-off.

DON'T stop and complain that your hands are aching; cup his genitals instead.

DO ask him for feedback about how you are doing — does he want it faster/slower?

DON'T forget to apply plenty of slippery lubrication to ease your movements.

DO vary your technique from massaging, twisting and rolling his penis to tugging his hair.

DON'T change your technique abruptly if he's clearly losing himself.

DO tease him by repeatedly building up the pressure then slowing right down.

DON'T change your rhythm or pressure as he moves to orgasm and ejaculation.

DO increase everything significantly seconds before he comes then go slowly.

DON'T pull faces or fuss about cleaning up.

Lovers tip

Whenever you have a spare half an hour while your baby is in the land of nod, forget the washing-up and give oral sex to each other instead. It's is a perfect way to pass the time. Flip a coin to decide whose turn it will be today or maybe you'd prefer a 69, that's both of you giving and receiving at once.

I have heard from many mums that the worst part of giving oral sex to their partners is swallowing their ejaculate. Be aware that if you develop this phobia during pregnancy it could hang around, conveniently, for years. There are two solutions to this. The first is that you invite him to come over your breasts. This is easy to do if he is standing between your legs as you sit on the bed. Or you just swallow quickly without grimacing. It's a mind over matter situation. If the taste is really bad then something is wrong and maybe he needs to change his diet. Yes — everything that he eats will affect the taste of his ejaculate. Encourage him to eat strawberries and pineapple if he tastes a bit sour as this will sweeten him up. Of course it's your choice not to swallow. You could let him ejaculate in your mouth and subtly spit it out into a tissue without any fuss or moaning. What counts here is that you have an agreement about what you do so he isn't offended by your actions.

♀♂ **Couple time**

Practice makes perfect so there's no time to lose. Tease each other by working your way down your bodies, a lick here and a nibble there and oops, you've gone right past the genitals ... you'd better start again.

Add your hands to increase the excitement – one hand stimulating his perineum or her G spot and the other searching out pleasure around the body.

Lick long and slow around her clitoris or his testicles, then increase the speed.

Play with holding an ice cube in your mouth then swig hot tea to experiment with the temperature.

Blow warm breath along his shaft or her labia lips (not into the vagina).

Put a well-lubricated finger into the anus as orgasm nears (always ask first).

Keep a regular rhythm and pressure during orgasm and don't stop until instructed.

You could always sit on the 'Cone' to increase your sexual tension as you perform oral sex. A Cone is an ultra-modern sex toy that is, you guessed it, shaped like a cone. It has a flat bottom which enables it to stand alone on the bed, the floor and it even has a suction pad so that you can stick it to the wall. The great thing about this toy is that it doesn't require hands to hold it in place and it offers clitoral, perineum and shallow vaginal stimulation. You can even practise squeezing your PC muscles around it. Now that's multitasking!

INTERCOURSE

At long last, we have come to the rightful place in this chapter for intercourse. That is after an extensive repertoire of foreplay, which has included talking, holding hands, kissing stroking, licking and pleasuring. I hope that you have revisited old techniques and developed new ones and shared really great lovemaking that didn't always need to include penetration.

♂ **His tip**
Please avoid pushing your partner's head down on to your penis in a moment of high passion. It will really put her off and could make her gag, which will turn you off too.

As you regain your confidence and desire for penetrative sex, remember to check whether you are feeling aroused and ready for intercourse before you begin. Decide which position you would feel most comfortable with; this process will also increase your mental and physical relaxation. Being on top of your partner will give you more of a sense of being in control and able to shift around. A cushion under your bottom and hips should enable penetration to occur without putting pressure on any scar tissue around the perineum. He should support himself with his arms so as not to put pressure on your breasts. Lie on your back at the edge of the bed, legs wide and him kneeling between them on the floor in front of you and this will avoid putting pressure on your Caesarean scar.

You may be curious about how tight you are after giving birth. One new dad told his partner that she was 75 per cent back to normal the first time that they made love after birth. She looked disappointed at this. He reassured her that he was talking about her vaginal tightness not how pleasurable it was for him.

If you've had stitches, it would be quite natural for you to tense up for fear of feeling pain. Try to relax your pelvic floor muscles, imagine that you are bulging them out so that your labia becomes soft and velvety, especially as you become more aroused. Use lots of extra lubrication so that you are wet and slippery. Encourage your partner to slow down and wait to be invited into your vagina, rather than him thrusting in. A good position to try here is with you on your back, bottom raised and him kneeling between your legs. You can give him gentle squeezes with your PC muscles as he rests the head of his penis between your labia lips awaiting your invitation. Ask him to make minimal movements inside your vagina whilst you assess how you are feeling inside. You can practise squeezing and releasing your muscles around his penis – there's no nicer exercise for your muscles than this.

I hope that by six months, the potential for painful intercourse will be minimal. If you do experience pain or tightness, it is vital that you see a doctor. By now your desire to try out new positions will have probably increased. I suggest that you buy yourself a book on modern day kama sutra and work your way through it. Remember that you need to be really excited before you go for it and don't rely on intercourse alone to give you an orgasm. Penetrative sex does many things

♀♂ Couple time

Try the coital alignment technique which aims to keep pressure and maximum pleasure on the clitoris by pushing your hips together. Lie on your backs and scissor your legs together. Let him penetrate you, then hold hands to help adjust your positions for perfect alignment. When you feel like a good fit together, you'll know that you have this one sorted.

for your relationship; it develops your trust and intimacy especially if you maintain eye contact. Choose positions that increase the contact between the penis and the anterior wall of the vagina where the G spot is, for example, having sex from behind with you on all fours, doggie style. Try to manually stimulate your clitoris and breasts, as this will increase your excitement. This is easy to do in any on-top position and this is also an ideal way to control the depth and rhythm of his penis inside you. Be imaginative in your choice of position but also with your location for sex. Try making love upright on the stairs or straddle him, leaning your back against his chest as he relaxes onto the wall of the shower.

 Lovers tip

Try to resist seeing sex as goal orientated around having an orgasm. Simply being inside your partner is a beautiful and connecting experience and if you're able to synchronise your breathing together, this will really deepen your intimacy. This means that you breathe in and out at the same time as each other whilst having sex. Most people fall around in a fit of giggles when they first try to do this but it's like learning to juggle, once you can do it, you always will.

6

Month Five

I imagine that by now, you are emerging from the chaos of the early months of motherhood and beginning to establish routines with your baby. Hopefully you'll be feeling physically recovered from the birth and stronger in your body too. Also, as most babies sleep for longer these days, you'll have more opportunity to take the time for yourself in the many ways that I've suggested in previous chapters. This chapter offers you new and exciting ways to deepen your intimate connection with your partner and gently challenges you to step more into your new role as the fantastic mum that you are.

On a bad day, you can feel pretty down about yourself and confused about who you are and how you fit in to society. It's natural to have doubts about everything and anything during these early months. If you didn't ask questions, how would you ever transform into this new beautiful mum that you are? We make the mistake of comparing ourselves to other new mums, whether they are friends, strangers on the street or magazine cut-outs. It's to our peril that we find ourselves believing that other mums are doing better that we are. So many new mums tell me that this is how they see it: every other new mum seems better presented – no sick on their shoulders or milky stains on their tops. Their stomach has gone back quicker than ours, their clothes fit them and they look sexy. Their baby is clearly sleeping through the night, doesn't scream in the street and is wearing freshly laundered clothes. Obviously, she is doing a better job as a domestic goddess than we are. She also smiles and laughs and looks like she is enjoying herself. She's not permanently frowning at people or avoiding their gaze.

I want to let you in on a secret: this mum doesn't exist. Nobody can be this perfect so don't kid yourself. Or rather, don't beat yourself up with this idea. Most women who appear to have it together in the outside world aren't like this in reality. We will never know what goes on once they close their front door. Maybe her life is like that dysfunctional soap opera family after all? And I bet she suffers from these random feelings of guilt like the rest of us do.

'SUPER MUM'

If you had been told when you gave birth that you would strive to be a 'super mum', you would probably have laughed out loud. Yet as you try to juggle your busy life with raising children, that's exactly what is happening. We can set ourselves such high expectations of how we should be as mums that we have a long way to fall if we can't live up to these. We land with a bang, assess the damage then try to scrabble back up and guess what? The cycle begins again. Yes, most of us are fantastic warriors, especially when it comes to doing stuff for our children but the cost of this is usually our sanity. We get emotionally rung out trying to keep up with our friends and their 'good parenting habits' or trying to do as we are told in the latest baby book.

Stop reading this book immediately and put your feet up. Trust that you know instinctively what to do with your baby. You are a mother now and a big prize of childbirth is meeting your innate wisdom. But you won't benefit from this if you're not quiet enough to hear it. Stop doubting your natural ability as a mum and don't believe it when you see a 'perfect mum' in the street. Have a little smile to yourself instead. This will give you an injection of energy and remember that you are doing the very best that you can do at this time and that's what counts.

'SUPER COOK'

Are you pushing yourself to be a super cook and housewife too? It's quite common to feel that there's little else for you to succeed at once you have got your baby organised for the day. Until you became a mum, many of you would have had a job that gave you a sense of success and purpose. So what has happened to that energy now? It is most likely that you are using it to turn yourself into this domestic goddess, which may or may not be a comfortable place for you to be. It could also be that you're wasting precious energy by feeling extremely guilty for not doing a better job around the house. Or you imagine that your partner expects you to do a better job and that he must wonder what you do all day, if you're not polishing the bathroom taps. Have you noticed that this is a no-win situation? If there was a pill that got us to do the housework and have orgasms, I'm sure that we would all be taking it. But there isn't. As I see it, you have the choice to take the easy way here, drop the guilt and choose a more relaxed approach to the housework.

I suggest that you sit down with your partner and talk these feelings through together. You may be surprised how little he has noticed or even considered this scenario that's now running away in your head. Regardless, he needs to be able to listen and help you to find a solution. This could be that you hire a cleaner if you can afford it or agree to share the housework. By doing this, you are both acknowledging that looking after the baby is a full-time job and in your 'free time' you need to relax rather than work in the house. There are many creative projects that you will be able to do with this extra energy.

'SUPER LOVER'

Are you struggling these last months to keep up your status as 'super lover' with your partner? Do you feel under pressure to be mother by day and lover by night? Be honest with yourself at least. It's normal to have these expectations of ourselves. Wouldn't it be perfect if we could put our babies to bed, then miraculously transform into sexy divas, ready to dance the night away with our partners? This fantasy is food for our dreams but quite frankly it wastes energy as it isn't going to happen like this. We may panic about when and how we will ever feel sexy again, especially on days when the tiredness is overwhelming. If only there was a magic button to press that could transform you. However, the truth we all have to face is that we will feel sexy when we're ready, which is when mind, body and spirit are in sync. Yes, you can help yourself to feel like this more often, but in between times, try to accept yourself for how you feel today. We put more pressure on ourselves personally as new mothers to be sexy, than all the partners, friends and media combined. Don't waste energy beating yourself up over something that is natural.

Whenever you feel under pressure from your own internal dialogue to be hot and sexy, do something kind for yourself, like buying a bunch of beautiful flowers. When your partner asks you who's been buying you flowers, dare to tell him that they are from your admirer. Before he explodes or implodes, explain to him that the admirer is you. This may open a door for you to talk with him about this pressure that you are putting on yourself to be sexy. Remember not to blame him for the way you are feeling. It helps to say, 'When you do this, I feel like this,' rather than pointing the finger with, 'You make me feel like this'. He will be a lot more receptive and supportive to what you are saying and this alone will help to boost your self-esteem.

'Super friend'

Have you been a 'super friend' these last months, particularly to your old friends from your old life? Do you feel that your friendships are in balance? Have you been trying harder to keep in touch than they have or are you feeling guilty that you haven't returned their calls? Remember that you are the one whose life has turned upside down. To the outside world, you have just had a baby. It's not going to help you to slink around feeling resentful to any of your so-called friends who haven't noticed that you've changed. If you don't tell them honestly how you are, they will never know. Be aware also of how much time you give to your new mum friends and be aware of the ones that are always asking for your ear but are never available to reciprocate. This may seem quite hard line but you only have time and space in your busy life for relation-ships that are mutually satisfying. If you find yourself feeling 'satisfied' by being the agony aunt for the post-natal group, I'd challenge you to think about this as your future career as you would be paid for your time and energy at least.

Take five minutes to write a list of all the friends who you would love to have around you today. These are the ones who you enjoy being with and who don't make you feel tired to be around. The best way to know this is how you feel, after you've spent time with them. Take another five minutes and write a list of the friends that you keep in your life because you feel that you should, through duty and feelings of guilt. Decide which group of friends you would prefer to keep in your heart and let the others go merrily on their way. This may seem ruthless but you need to be this way for survival in this new world of being a mother. This is preparation for all the parents that will cross your path on your journey through motherhood. If you were to make them all friends, you would be exhausted. You'd be constantly giving and doing things for others rather than taking care of yourself. Remember to use the email as much as possible for communication, especially for practical matters. It's a perfect forum for mothers to keep in touch.

CLUTTER

De-clutter your life. This should be a big theme for you this month, as I imagine that by now, you are feeling drowned by ever-increasing baby things, old clothes and unopened mail.

It can be very depressing to be surrounded by clutter in our everyday lives and I have heard from many mums that this was a big factor in why they felt claustrophobic at home. You will only feel the benefits if you do it and I recommend that you set yourself the task of decreasing your possessions by one third this month.

♀♂ Couple time

I urge you to de-clutter together as you will be able to encourage each other to let go of those prized possessions. A rule of thumb would be, if you haven't worn it or used it for 18 months then it should go to the charity shop or a friend or relative. I am not recommending that you dump the things as this adds to the potential of future environmental catastrophes in your baby's lifetime. Go together, room by room, beginning with your bedroom.

Your bedroom has the potential to be the biggest dumping ground in your home. This isn't a good idea as your bedroom is where you have your private intimate relationship and it is your space. Put the baby things into your baby's room, box up small baby clothes or pass them on and put the baby books on the bookshelves elsewhere. If you haven't moved your baby into his own room yet, this may be a good moment to consider it. Nobody can tell you when to do this but you will notice how much space you gain when you do. Most couples also report an increase in their physical intimacy as it seems that even though the house is your oyster, so to speak, most people still feel most sexual when they go to bed together without the watchful eye of their baby.

Take a look in your wardrobe; it would be great if you could get rid of ten items of clothing immediately.

It's tempting to look at your pre-pregnancy clothes and feel depressed that you will never be able to get back into them, but that won't necessarily be the case. What is more relevant is that you may no longer feel like the person who wore them before, especially if you are a first-time mum. Try them on and see how comfortable you feel. Ask your partner for his opinion and be as ruthless as you can.

Be aware that replacing these cast-offs with loose-fitting clothes and tracksuits is not an ideal exchange. Even though you need to dress in practical, child-friendly clothes, you will not be helping yourself to feel good and eventually sexy, if you dress sloppily. Choose to wear something because it feels comfortable, soft and relaxing by all means, as this will help you to feel the same. Just be sure that it's not oversized and washed out.

The following are tips on how to look and feel good from other mums. They're in no particular order but I have scored them based on the amount of effort they could take on an average tired day and the level of boost to your self-esteem. (10 is the most effort and the best score.)

- Make an effort to get dressed in clean clothes, even if you are only going to the supermarket.
  Effort: 3 / Gain: 6 (especially if you bump into people you know)

- Put on your jewellery and perfume to sit down to dinner with your partner.
  Effort: 1 / Gain: 8 (it's amazing the lift a pair of pearl earrings gives you)

- Ban black – wear soft, bright colours instead.
  Effort: 4 / Gain: 7 (these colours will brighten your complexion even on tired days)

- Buy the most expensive pair of jeans you can afford.
  Effort: 5 / Gain: 9 (you will never regret this one – your bottom will look great)

The New Mum's Guide to Sex

- Shop for accessories, handbags, shoes, jewellery and lipsticks.
  Effort: 5 / Gain: 9 (these will have life beyond the post-natal months)

- Invest in a good quality moisturiser and hand cream.
  Effort: 2 / Gain: 10 (pleasure from rubbing it in, pleasure from the results)

- Buy ten T-shirts — same brand, different colours.
  Effort: 3 / Gain: 8 (these will mix and match with your existing wardrobe)

- Have your hair cut and styled every couple of months.
  Effort: 4 / Gain: 10 (you will see a new you appearing in the mirror)

- Don't try to squeeze into clothes that are obviously too small for you.
  Effort: 10 (if you do) / Gain: 10 (if you don't) (you may be back in them soon)

- If you wear make-up, put it on and brush your hair every morning.
  Effort: 6 / Gain: 9 (you will feel better for this and so will your baby)

You wouldn't be the first new mum to feel like going on a shopping splurge to buy new outfits or even a complete new wardrobe. My best advice would be to go shopping with an older and wiser friend rather than another new mum. If you have enough money, I would recommend that you have a personal shopper. You need someone who is not submerged in babyhood to be able to see your potential and to tell you the truth about what looks good. Remember that it may take up to a year for you to regain your natural shape, so be gentle on yourself.

♂ **His tip**

You could also benefit from getting rid of your old clothes. Ask your partner to review your clothes with you and tell you what she really likes you in and what she doesn't. Try not to take it to heart or try to retaliate when she asks you for your opinion on her clothes. Enjoy the fact that she is giving you her undivided attention.

Food

Time to de-clutter the kitchen and take stock of your diet. When I say that word – diet – I'm not suggesting that you should go on an actual diet. Not so soon after giving birth and especially not if you are still breastfeeding. However, it is high time to draw your attention to the food that you are putting in your mouth. You know that expression, 'a moment on your lips, a lifetime on your hips'. Well, it does have some validity, doesn't it? You may need a fresh start to break some of these old patterns, like biscuits with tea, an extra slice of toast and jam mid-morning or a bowl of cereal before bed. By clearing out your kitchen cupboards and fridge, you will be able to do this.

♀♂ Couple time

If you have the opportunity to go shopping with your partner then head for the best department store in town. Here you will generally find a very baby-friendly environment. However, don't go to the baby department but enjoy looking at the soft furnishings, bed covers, scented candles, soft towels and underwear and anything else that makes your dreams of luxury and romance come true. See if you can find an object for each of your senses: touch, taste, see, smell and hear. What's important is to share this time together talking and dreaming about your life together.

If you are already squirming at the thought of this, then you need to wake up to the reality that ready made food is not going to keep you healthy and strong or get you back into great shape as quickly as you would like. I'm talking to you both now. If you would like more information about diet and nutrition, look in the resources section for recommended reading.

From what I have seen with my clients over the years and from my own personal experience, I believe that our diet should be as natural, simple and include as many high quality, preferably organic fruit and vegetables as possible. If we eat too many high-fat, high-sugar, salty foods then we risk losing control of our health and shape. We all want to feel that we are doing the best for our bodies by feeding them well. But we need to be realistic; it's easy for these good intentions to break down, especially at times of stress. So, forgive yourself if this has been you and turn over a new leaf from today.

———————

Put a reminder on the fridge that reminds you to think about what you are taking out of it to eat. Or, as a second-time mum suggested, instead substitute it with a photo of yourself when you were at your largest during your first pregnancy. This will motivate you to stay awake and alert about what you are eating.

As you wipe out the cupboard shelves, imagine filling them with wonderful nutritious food that will help you to feel and look great from the inside out. If all you can think about these days is what to feed your baby, then I want to give you a gentle nudge to remind you not to forget about your own diet in this process.

Why not stock up on foods that will stimulate your sexual desire? Did you know that when you eat foods that aren't good for you, you are potentially decreasing your libido, as what you eat has a direct effect on your hormones? You may be deficient in significant nutrients that your body

♀♂ Couple time

Take your time to work together through the kitchen cupboards and the fridge, checking the use-by dates and contents of packets and tins as you go. You should aim to keep all the natural produce like rice, pasta, noodles, dried beans and lentils and give away anything that is ready made with additives and a high salt content. These products may have been helpful to you over the past few months as you juggled cooking with a small baby but you can do better than this now. Freshly made food from natural ingredients is best for all of us.

needs, especially if this is a second or subsequent pregnancy. Sometimes you cannot replace all your body's requirements through your diet alone and you would be best advised to visit a nutritionist who will give you what your body needs. We can waste a lot of money buying supplements that we read about in magazines or hear about from friends. Be practical and get advice from an expert, as this will save you time and money in the long run.

Sexy foods

I am not recommending that you eat exclusively from this list but try to incorporate a little of these natural ingredients into your everyday meals:

apples
artichokes
asparagus
avocados
bananas
beetroot
blackberries
blueberries
Brazil nuts
brown rice
cardamom
celery
cheese
cherries
cinnamon
dates

fennel
figs
garlic
ginger
gooseberries
hazelnuts
leeks
liquorice
mangos
nori seaweed
nutmeg
oats
onions
parsley
pomegranates
pumpkin

pumpkin seeds
quinoa
raspberries
sesame seeds
soaked seeds
spinach
steamed kale
strawberries
sunflower seeds
tomatoes
trout
turmeric
vanilla
watercress
wild salmon

My advice is to keep your menu simple and keep the alcohol to a minimum, else you may fall a sleep before the dessert. More tips for on the day that you can divide between you:

- Tuck your baby into bed and ask him to sleep through the night tonight.

- Do a quick tidy of the house.

- Take a shower and dress up in your sexiest clothes.

- Set the table together and include fresh flowers and candles.

- Select some music to suit both your tastes.

♀♂ Couple time

Decide to have a romantic meal together and cook a menu that includes these ingredients. Spend time planning what you are going to eat together, then shop for the ingredients, cook it together and clear up together. Take your time with the planning phase as this will help to increase your appetite. You could even prepare some of the food the day before. This is meant to be fun, not hard work. It will also force you to break your domestic patterns of who shops, who cooks, and who washes up. Hopefully you will laugh a lot together while doing this.

> ♂ **His tip**
> Please don't say that you can't or won't cook, or that you find it boring. See it as fun rather than a chore.

I suggest that one of you takes charge of the starter and dessert and the other the main course. This doesn't mean that you can't help each other with preparation but it means that only one of you is the head chef and serving the food to the table for the other. So head chef, pay attention to how you serve the food. Lay it out so it looks beautiful on the plates. Really appreciate all the colours and textures and flavours. For dessert, why don't you enjoy feeding each other some splendid fruits dipped in chocolate on cocktail sticks? And to increase your delight, surprise him by blindfolding each other. If you're feeling adventurous you could involve your whole body and get him to guess which part you are feeding him from. Be brave and add a few extras like ice cubes.

Once you've finished eating, put on your favourite music and dance together or even dance for each other. Try doing a striptease for him — you can become that sexy dancing diva in your own home tonight. Wash up in the morning.

♀♂ **Couple tip**

Go through cookery books together and choose
a menu that is easy to cook and full of delicious
and fresh ingredients.

DANCING

If you enjoy dancing or even if you felt a little shy in front of
each other, why not consider taking up dance classes? You can
do this together or separately. It's a perfect way to get into
shape. There's lots of choice from belly-dancing to salsa and
burlesque and even pole dancing. I've seen transformations
not only in the shape of mums who have started to dance but
more in the way they feel about themselves. It has boosted
their self-confidence, they feel sexy when they're dancing and
this feeling continues to dance through their week. There are
recommendations for this in the resources section.

 Lovers tip

You can hire a private teacher to come and teach
you to dance in your own home. Dancing in rhythm
together will help you to be more aligned in your
life and particularly in the bedroom.

Of course you can play your favourite music at home and have a bop around, it beats vacuuming any day and your baby will love to watch you. Draw the curtains, to be sure that you're not performing in front of your neighbours, then let your hair down to the music. Gyrate your hips, swing your bottom, rock your pelvis and sashay around. Let the music move you. Do this every day for five minutes and you will be transformed.

Transformed into what? Well, you may just want to gain a little extra energy to cope with your daily life or you may want to re-sculpt your body into a toned goddess. But before we get carried away, let's remember that you are still less than half a year after giving birth and you still may not be completely recovered. Many mums are still experiencing pain in their pelvis or working to realign their stomach muscles. So please don't overexert yourself. Check out how your body feels from the inside first. There's no competition to get back into shape, although the competition is probably going on inside your head as you read this.

Take a measured approach to getting your figure back, let the natural healing happen in the early months and watch how nature takes it course, helping your uterus and stomach to shrink down. Be kind to yourself about the way your body looks but in the same breath don't be lazy. It's too easy to stay on the sofa and imagine yourself jogging around the park when it's warmer or when you have the right training shoes or when you've lost a few pounds to stave off any embarrassment. Plan today to take little tiny steps to feeling great about yourself. Join a gym that has a crèche and preferably a swimming pool (and go at least twice a week) or locate a local mum and baby-jogging group (but resist going for coffee and cake after). Gone are the days when you were housebound with your baby. Remember that every time you exercise, you release endorphins that not only make you feel great but they also strengthen your immune system and boost your libido.

♀♂ **Couple tip**

Going to the gym together and putting your baby in the crèche will be very valuable time spent together.

Did you get around to doing the mirror exercise that I suggested in Chapter 3 or did you give away all the mirrors in the house when you de-cluttered? It does take confidence to take your clothes off, especially as the post-natal months tick on, but I encourage you to do it and have a really good, loving look at yourself. Body confidence is a buzz word of our time, yet it is a vital ingredient of how sexually confident we feel. So where can you buy it, and how much does it cost?

The unfortunate answer is that either we have it or we don't. If you don't or if you've just temporarily lost it since giving birth, read on through the next pages, to help you to reclaim it.

There's no better mirror than your partner when it comes to seeing the beauty of your body. Dare to stand naked in front of each other and admire what you see. Be brave and try not to collapse into a fit of giggles. See if you can say five positive things about his or her body and don't argue or disagree with what they say. You may be surprised.

♂ **His tip**

Let her know with your eyes and gestures how beautiful she is. Explain that how good she feels about herself will shine out of her. When she has positive thoughts about her body you can see it in her body posture and movements. You may not be conscious of this but look more closely now, so that you can congratulate her whenever she shows you that she is feeling good about herself.

Our main enemy to look out for is our minds. It's our internal dialogues that stop us from absorbing all the positive feedback that our partners give us. These negative words are constantly chattering to you over your shoulder, saying things like, 'You're not good enough', 'He's just saying that', 'You're really a dumpling', etc. We have a choice to let them run our lives or banish them. Even on the days when you feel most tired, you can still assert this choice. Your mind will initially put up a fight but I challenge you to persist so that you are only playing the tapes that you have selected in your head every day. The mind needs training just like our bodies. Why? Well, if you use it well, it will be the key to turning your sex light back on. Ignore it, and I bet that it will continue to scream obscenities at you for years to come.

You have the power in your mind to change the way you look, feel and act. Start imaging yourself as the woman you dream to be in all her aspects. Tell your body how it will look and how it will move and so on. I guarantee you that this approach will work as experiments have shown that the power of thought alone can develop body muscles.

Begin to visualise your stomach muscles tightening, excess water draining out of your body and your bottom and hips shrinking back to their pre-pregnancy shape and size or even smaller.

AFFIRMATIONS

You can add another layer to your mind-control by doing affirmations. These are sentences or words that you choose because you aspire to be or act a certain way. Unfortunately, we often sabotage this because of our negative self-concepts. Here are a few suggestions:

• I'm a beautiful mummy.

• I'm sexy and happy and beautiful.

• I love the way I look today.

• Even though I'm tired, I'm making an effort to make the most of myself.

Make up your own and stick them on to the fridge, the dashboard, by your bed and remember to read them out loud or to yourself as much as possible. Your baby will also be really happy to hear them.

The easiest way to achieve a clear mind is through meditation but if this wasn't your natural path before becoming a mum it may not be for you. However, before you give up, remember that all of life is a meditation and that everything you do can become a meditation, like vacuuming, washing-up and even ironing. Whenever I want to really think about something, I'll wipe down the kitchen cupboards or clean the sink. Bizarre but it connects me to my creativity. There is no doubt that the more space we can create in our minds, the more place there is for being positive.

I do strongly suggest that you try to find a mother and baby yoga class, as this is a wonderful way to stretch out your body and find a little inner peace. This is most achievable if you can find a class that includes baby massage first. Alternatively, practise yoga or Pilates either from a book or DVD at home for ten minutes each day. Try to lie down on the floor after you have done this and practise breathing. Focus on taking a long slow breath in through your nose and filling your belly with air, you should see it rising, then let your breath slowly release through your mouth as if you are blowing out of a straw. Repeat this three times then say your positive affirmation to yourself. It should be something like, 'I am a beautiful, sexy mummy and I deserve to relax.' Saying it is believing it and soon you'll feel it right through your body. Get up slowly and drink a glass of water. Notice how relaxed and wonderful you feel. This is a much better way to approach the daily chores.

From my own personal experience, I benefited enormously from doing a daily yoga practice at home, especially through the early years of raising my children. Yes, it took discipline and determination, especially when I had broken nights but the energy that I gained outweighed this. Not only did I gain physical strength and flexibility, I also found that over time, I became less frazzled by the constant demands of my children. But what I really wanted to share with you was how it took me back into my pelvis and helped to reignite my sexual fire from inside my own body. This would happen as I lay on the floor to integrate the postures that I had done. I felt my body moving in ways that naturally connected me with my sexual energy. These were the movements:

1. Put your feet flat on the floor and bend your knees.
2. Gently begin to bounce your pelvis up and down. Stay connected with the movement and allow the bouncing to develop its own rhythm and speed. Keep moving until you feel the heat building in your pelvis.
3. Next, carefully let your knees drop towards the floor and keep the soles of your feet together. Do not push your knees out; let them find their natural open point.
4. Stay with the feelings or heat or nothingness in your pelvis and relax. Let any sensations be carried with your breath up your body to your chest.

When I did this, I was eventually able to imagine a fire burning in my pelvis and rising through my body but this takes time and practice.

If you find that every time you lie on the floor you are fighting off falling asleep then try having a catnap when your baby next sleeps. I have seen fantastic results with mums who have taken a power nap every day rather than a long sleep. It seems that 20 to 30 minutes is the optimum time and I recommend that you use a 'catnapper' CD for this (see the resources for more

♂ **His tip**

Ask your partner about this 'catnapper' CD, especially if you are feeling exhausted from broken nights or you are travelling a lot. Never underestimate the impact that sleep-deprivation may be having on your mood or on your partner's emotions. It's easy to become a monster, especially at 3 am in the morning. It is no coincidence that sleep-deprivation is a torture technique. I promise you that as soon as your baby sleeps through the night, you will see a transformation in both your personalities. This time will pass and hopefully you will look back on it with humour.

information). This will take you in and out of a deep sleep in just 30 minutes. In this way you will have time to do other things for yourself before your baby wakes up.

Sleep also helps us to lose weight, have fantastic skin and improve our mood and sexual desire so my advice is to have several of these catnaps a day.

Many couples swear by their daily or weekly yoga practice as it helps them to cope with their crazy lives. It helps the

Lovers tip

As you find yourselves able to access deeper levels of relaxation, so your body will become attuned to finer sensations too. Try exploring your senses together. Keep it simple; it doesn't have to be elaborate.

Your visual senses can be awakened by making love with your eyes open, by watching him caress your body or by tracing the outline of his facial features.

Your listening senses can be awakened by listening to the sounds you make from pleasure, by putting your head on his chest and listening to his heartbeat or by playing sensual music in the background as you make love.

Your taste senses can be awakened by licking chocolate or yogurt off your most private body parts, by tasting the salty sweat of your passion or by sucking a hot, mint sweet as you have oral sex.

Your touch senses can be awakened by blowing a feather-light breath over his body, by stroking each other with soft fabrics or by touching each other erotically with your softly oiled hands.

mind to be still and the body to be flexible. These are both ideal qualities for a healthy sex life. If you can integrate yoga-type breathing into your lovemaking, especially before or during intercourse, you will notice how much more deeply you are able to connect with each other. See resources for recommended reading. Physical flexibility will help you to experiment more with unusual sexual positions.

♀♂ **Couple time**

Practise breathing together – this will beat arguing at 6 am and is a very relaxing way to connect with each other. Especially when you have both had hectic days but would like to find a place to connect quickly and easily. It also reminds you to pay attention to your own breathing patterns. Try lying facing each other on your sides and have your eyes open so that you can gaze at each other whilst you breathe together. As you breathe in through your nose, imagine your breath filling your chest and your heart. As you breathe out through your mouth, imagine your breath flowing into your partner's heart and chest. You could also imagine your partner's breath coming into your heart from their heart as you breathe in. Repeat this for three to five breaths. This sounds more complicated than it is so be daring and give it a go.

7

Month Six

Congratulations, you've made it to your half birthday. I expect you can't believe how quickly the time has flown by, no parent ever can. So much has changed for you both in just a little more than a year. Blink and you risk missing the magical and sometimes daily changes in your baby: from a babe in your arms to a little person, beaming out smiles, eating solid food and hopefully sleeping through the night, or most of it at least. I'm not wishing his life away, but each of these tiny developmental stages, is a step towards his independence and to yours too. Have you noticed that life isn't quite as stressful and bizarre as it was just six months ago? You're on the point of crossing a threshold and it's worth stopping for a moment to recognise and celebrate this achievement.

Hopefully, you will have noticed an increase in your energy if you've recently given up or even reduced breastfeeding. Most mums feel that they finally get their bodies back after nine months of pregnancy and six months (or more) of feeding your baby. You may lose weight, regain your figure and your bra size and hopefully feel an immediate surge in your libido. However, there are no guarantees that this will be the way for you. Like all pregnancy and post-natal 'symptoms', you'll find your own path through this period of change. Try to be patient with your body as it makes the necessary hormonal adjustments, which can sometimes feel a little like going from fifth gear to reverse. One of the best ways to regain hormonal balance is to do daily exercise – even a walk around the park is better than nothing. There are also many supplements that help you to balance your hormones and I have included references for these in the resources section.

I'm wondering if you've even noticed that you have gained time or energy? Perhaps you've already filled this time with projects or chores without acknowledging its existence? You wouldn't be alone if you have, as it seems to be part of our nature as mothers to nurture others before ourselves. I see this happening everywhere, regardless of our cultural background. We can be run ragged looking after other people and we don't even realise that we are doing it, as it's such an ingrained pattern. If I asked you to draw a pie chart to represent the things you do for yourself versus the things you do for others, how big would your slice be? Would it be wafer thin or generously proportioned? Of course there is no question that your baby deserves to have a healthy piece of the pie, but do you need to feed your partner, family and friends so well? And if you are preparing to go back to work in the next months, be aware that your commitment to your job is going to gobble up even more of your slice of pie.

If you are going to go back to work in the next weeks or months, begin to put a list of sexy, self-nurturing habits into your life. These will be activities that you may dream about doing but that you can't imagine ever finding time to do. Change this belief and even if you're not planning on returning to work, do these anyway.

Here are a few examples:

• Have a sensual massage once a month.

• Read a sexy or romantic novel, anywhere but at home.

• Go to the movies to watch a romantic film.

• Watch other couples kissing.

• Sit in a café and write down the erotic details of how you conceived your baby.

• Go out for a walk in nature, at least once a week.

The main thrust of this chapter is to encourage you to have strategies that help you to avoid being rung out in your life as a mother. Even though it's early days in your family life, it is never too early to put yourself at the top of the list for your attention. Whenever you get exhausted from overworking, overdoing or over-giving, you'll be starving yourself of a really yummy piece of pie, the sexy slice, as this is so often the first thing to disappear from your life when you overdo it. Sexuality isn't just about making love with your partner or dressing like a sexy diva, although these are both excellent ideas. It's also about reconnecting with the flame that burns inside you and sparks you up in life. Do you recognise the part that I'm talking about? Like all fires, you'll need to fan the flames by doing things that feed you. It's the same deal with the fire in your relationship; you both need commitment to feeding it with your love and tenderness to keep it burning bright. Even when you're having bad times together, a low burning fire is better than no fire – it's always easier to reignite embers than a completely dead fire.

Resentment is often the culprit for bad times in our intimate relationships. Something that may have begun life as a tiny hint of resentment, once left unspoken, can easily grow into a resentment monster that wreaks havoc in our partnership. It's usually the small stuff, that doesn't seem significant enough to talk about, but it adds up over the years and eventually creates big trouble. This dynamic can be the reason why some women lose all interest in sex with their partners. They're just not able to get the resentment out of the bedroom. We need to look at how we juggle our domestic life. Who in your partnership does the cleaning, loads the dishwasher, folds up and puts away the washing and all the hundreds of other household chores? I'm continually amazed that children seem to increase the workload tenfold and how one of you will unconsciously take on more of the work than the other. It's only when you wake up to the reality that your beloved has his or her feet up, whilst you are still on yours, that the resentment creeps in. This scenario becomes more intense if Mum returns to work, as everything will be that much more tiring and stressful. You will need a military-style operation to get through your life.

♂ His tip

If your partner is going to return to work soon, please try to be extra considerate. She is going to be emotional about leaving the baby, possibly for the first time with a carer (even if it's you). From now on her attention and focus will be continually split between home and work and she will need help to run the house. Even if you can afford to pay for help, watch out. She needs to see that you are pulling your weight at home. If you bury your head in the sand, she will notice and resentment will build between you.

♀♂ **Couple tip**

Talk about how you are going to cope with any changes in your domestic life. Make a list of what needs to be done in the house and garden and review it every three months. This could involve drawing up a rota of what needs to be done every day, week and month. Go through each of the jobs and say why they are important to you individually. This gives you an opportunity to appreciate that a chore that may seem insignificant to you might be top priority for your partner. As your children grow, they will be able to play an active role in this schedule too.

A wonderful way to spice up this balance of power at home is to play a game where one of you is the dominant one and the other the passive one for a certain length of time, then you swap roles. If you're already thinking that there could be potential for sexual engagement in this idea, then you wouldn't be wrong, but there doesn't have to be. Let me give you an example of how other parents have approached this game.

One couple decided to spend a weekend in their roles. Dad went first as the passive partner, Mum the active partner and they decided to stay like this for three hours. You can do it for as long or little time as you like, so don't panic. Whilst Mum was active, she asked him to run her a bath, massage her feet and shoulders, do the vacuuming, peel the potatoes for dinner and sing a song. Quite an unusual collection of requests but they had lots of fun doing this together. Did you notice that all of these actions were child friendly, so there's no need to wait for baby's bedtime to play? Dad had a choice whether he wanted to do everything that Mum asked him to – keep in mind that you always have a choice to say no – but he was happy to play along. The next day, Dad was active and Mum was passive for another three hours. Dad asked Mum to help him to clean his car, make him tea and toast, sit with him silently while he read the newspaper, perform oral sex and read him a bedtime story. Happily for Dad, Mum fulfilled his wishes, some during the baby's nap time and others with the baby in tow.

Sex doesn't have to be limited to the bedroom or to bedtime. For a busy mum, the one place she finds maximum peace and quiet is in her bed at night. The feeling of lying down in warm and snugly bed at the end of a long day cannot be beaten. Nothing should disturb this, although this will depend on how often or early the children wake up. Needless to say the bedroom can be the least sexy place in your house. Clothes piled up on the floor and any available furniture, dirty plates and cups and two-year-old

Sunday supplements scattered around. Get the picture? But if there's a will, there's a way to transform your bedroom from a dumping ground to an erotic paradise. Try the following:

- Put a lock on your bedroom door.

- Get a soft, velvety cover to transform your bed into a more sensuous place.

- Choose cushions for their beauty, comfort and to help you play around with positions.

- Keep a soft light on throughout your lovemaking.

- Buy candles with a sensual fragrance.

- Have a selection of music for relaxation (this will also filter out your love noises).

- Find a lockable cupboard for storage of your private toys.

- Keep a supply of massage oil/lubricant to hand.

One of the biggest complaints I hear from parents of children of all ages, is that they are just too tired for sex. It's no wonder, when most of us don't even get around to thinking about sex until after ten o'clock. This is too late in the day to have the energy or enthusiasm for sex and trying to get it on as you fall into bed exhausted, isn't a good idea. Yawning over your partner isn't a big turn-on either. Another regular feature of long-term relationships is that one of you may prefer sex at night whilst your partner wants it in the mornings. Sometimes, this situation can make you feel that the two of you are sexually incompatible, as you never want to have sex at the same time. This isn't necessarily true.

If you're finding yourself turning down his sexual advances, drop the guilt and focus on how to say so in a loving and constructive way. My suggestion would be to propose an alternative time when you are confident that you will have more energy. This will reassure him that you are still interested in him as your lover, just not at midnight.

 Lovers tip

You need to discover when your natural energy patterns are compatible. This involves finding out when you both have the most energy and inclination for sex within any 24-hour cycle. If this doesn't exist during your working week, then look for it during your weekends. I am confident that you will find some compatibility, even if it means that you set the alarm clock for 4 am.

> ♂ **His tip**
> Just because she isn't in the mood, doesn't mean that you can't be. What's important is that you don't insist that she engages with you sexually if she doesn't want to. Respect her wishes and she may feel comfortable with you lying in her arms, stroking each other, whilst you self-pleasure. You will never know how she will react to this suggestion, unless you ask her.

Try these:

• Set the alarm clock for 4 am.

• Have an afternoon siesta together.

• Come home for lunch together and be spontaneous.

• Set up a daytime meeting in a hotel.

• Go for a country walk and surprise each other.

Have you ever noticed how much time we spend trying to second-guess what our partners are thinking? It would be a whole lot simpler for everyone if we asked what was going on with him. Nothing beats good communication to iron out the creases in our relationships. Even if you find it difficult to communicate verbally with each other, try non-verbal communication. The way you look at each other will tell a story;

a gentle brush past with your arm gives a flicker of interest, pushing breasts against his body is a definite invitation and the wink of your eye sparks the potential for being naughty.

One hot subject that needs a mention here is faking orgasms, as this is non-verbal communication too (even if you make lots of noise). If we're honest, most women have considered it and some regularly do it, as it can be a good way to get sex over with quickly – especially if this late-night sex threatens to impinge on your precious sleep. It's not a bad thing to do, but it isn't the most truthful way. It can be tempting to get into a habit of faking orgasms, as this avoids you having to say what you want and don't want in bed. Try to tell your partner the truth, even if it means admitting that this way of making love isn't turning you on and that you don't know what would. There really is no place today for the concept that a woman has a duty to satisfy her partner.

The only duty we have as women, partners, mothers and lovers is to satisfy ourselves the best we can, with the resources we have at our disposal. This may mean that we have to shake our opinions around a little. Take orgasms for example, sometimes by faking one we can actually bring one on. You could call this 'fake it to make it', like many other women do.

To perfect this 'fake it to make it' method, you need to push the boat out with your performance – the louder the better. Squeeze your PC muscles rapidly for a count of 20. Breathe in strongly through your nose as if you are sucking up air through your vagina. Say yes powerfully on the exhalation. Replace all thoughts of shopping lists, washing or housework with the thought of pleasure and excitement. Squeeze your thighs and buttocks together and bounce your pelvis. With so much energy building in your pelvis you're bound to go pop.

It's no more our duty to sexually satisfy our partners, than it is to be full-time housekeepers. We're often complaining that we need to get out of our 'four walls' and this is a natural desire, as we do spend a substantial chunk of time at home, supporting and nurturing the family. Now imagine if we could turn this around and become desperate to get home to discover sexual, sensual pleasure in every room of our house. Our homes wouldn't be our domestic prisons. If we can open our minds and our imagination, they will become our temples of paradise. Read on.

If sex in the bedroom can be boring and predictable at times, then we need to search for other hidden places that fulfil our sexual dreams and fantasies, within the fabric of our home. Anywhere that feels a little naughty, like the kitchen counter, can really spice things up. This is easy to imagine whilst your children are small, but as they grow, it becomes increasingly difficult to envisage yourself being intimate anywhere but behind a locked door. The challenge is to train yourselves to prioritise your own emotional or physical satisfaction. This may mean organising for your children to be away from home, putting them to bed early or structuring your day to

♀♂ **Couple time**

Go around the house together like detectives, room by room, looking for potential pleasure zones. Enjoy your sexy banter and laughing together. Remember that this adventure is your secret as two consenting lovers, rather than parents.

Bathroom adventures begin by slipping and sliding together in the bath or shower. Soap each other down with an erotic shaped soap. Dry each other off with soft fluffy towels and massage each other with lotion, with the heating on high. Position a full size mirror where you can enjoy watching each other.

The best sex toy currently available for the bathroom is called the 'Rub my Duckie' (see the resources). It looks like a children's bath duck but vibrates from its beak and tail.

Sitting room adventures should spill on to the floor rather than rolling off the sofa. Have a soft rug and cushions of all shapes and sizes to prop you up and support you in your study of the modern day kama sutra together. Choose coffee table books with sensual photographs such as bodies, landscapes or whatever turns you on. Select three educational sex books for your bookshelf, a couple of his and hers sexy DVDs, an adult board game and some sexy CDs that you keep for private moments.

If you have a spare bedroom, transform it into your alter ego. Have fantasy dressing-up clothes in the wardrobe and vibrators shaped like nail varnish, lipstick and mascara out on the dressing table, ready for action. Put your sexy fantasy storybooks on the bedside table in case you want a little late-night private reading.

The kitchen is a pleasure dome with all the potential to awaken your senses from nibbling bananas, sucking grapes, sipping fresh juices, licking yogurt pots, experimenting with spices and playing with ice cubes. Always keep a pot of chocolate body paint in the fridge and a vanilla bondage kit in the cupboard.

Your garden offers you not just the potential for green fingers but hot fingers. Create a haven to lie naked together under the stars and moon and without being spotted by your neighbours. Set up a water feature and plant some highly scented flowers to heighten your sensations.

If you are struggling with the motivation to do any of this, then you wouldn't be alone. It takes a great deal of effort to be bothered, especially after a day of taking care of your baby. But I promise you that you can transform how you're feeling by allowing yourself to let your hair down and giving your imagination and fantasies permission to run wild.

ensure that you are home when they are not. This will then give you free access to your adult playground and introduce you to your 'Household Companion' for lifelong friendship and pleasure.

Fantasy

One way to cope with the everyday monotony of mother-hood is to give yourself permission to fantasise. It's a welcome escape from the mundaneness of your life and you don't even need to get off the sofa to do it. Choose your moment wisely, as you don't want to abandon your children when you slip away to your fantasy land. Breastfeeding, washing-up, iron-ing and vacuuming would be ideal times.

The mind is our best aphrodisiac and nobody knows or needs to know what is going on in there. Your fantasies are your private property and there's no need to share them with Dad or anyone for that matter. It's sometimes better that you don't, especially if they involve your mutual friends. Fantasising about your partner's boss putting you over his knee is best kept to yourself, unless you can be certain that it would be something that your partner would enjoy too and you can both distinguish between the fantasy and reality. Your fantasies will fire you up and light up your libido. They're good for your health and vitality, as are all good things that involve sex.

Don't even let yourself think for a moment that mums aren't allowed to fantasise because this is 100 per cent not true. It's more important now than ever that you loosen up your mind and your imagination. It's like going to the gym, the brain gym, which is fantastic if you're a mum who is often complaining that you've lost your brain since having a baby. Sometimes it's good to be in this dreamy, brainless zone, especially as we normally have a busy brain. If you'd like ideas you may be inspired by some collections of other women's fantasies in books such as *My Secret Garden* or *Women On Top*. See the resources for more information.

You may be surprised how similar your fantasies are to those of other women. There are no right or wrongs when it comes to what turns you on and as you are not living them in reality but in your head, nobody will give you feedback. The only rule is that you don't waste your time daydreaming too much about past or future events, as this just isn't productive.

It's like moaning in your head about your situation and then not doing anything to change it. Fantasies will distract you for a moment from the reality of your everyday life, but it's up to you how you manage them.

Take the scenario of the plumber coming round to service more than just the boiler or the next time you push the pram around the park you could visualise rolling in the long grass with a stranger. You could visit these for as little or as long a time as you have available, teasing yourself with the idea, then allowing the story to unfold in your mind as the day goes by.

Fantasies can really help to spice up your sex life with your partner even if they're in your head rather than on your lips. Some mums feel that their fantasies have played a role in keeping their relationship together during bad times. You're not breaking any rules if you don't tell him that you're imagining that he's Dr Brown, or that you're on your first date again, or that he's a complete stranger. What counts is that you can't keep your hot hands off him.

If the idea of sharing your fantasies with him is just a stretch too far, be reassured, that should you decide to spill the beans one day, then there's very little chance that they won't be welcome. It's our own beliefs about what mothers should and shouldn't do that trips us up. We often sabotage our potential, especially in the sexual arena. Take a fantasy in which you are the beautiful heroine who's swept off her feet by the knight in shining armour. Just perfect, until you

♀♂ **Couple time**

Decide that you are going to create a fantasy story together. It may be that you build it up over time, letting it gain momentum between you. One of you sets the scene and then you take it in turns to add to the story. It's great fun to do this by email, especially if you're away on business. It will certainly whet your appetite for your return. You could even read it out to each other in bed. Why should the children have all the bedtime stories?

The fantasies that you share together are your private property as lovers. They have the potential to spark you up in an instant, which as time poor parents can be very handy. Always seize the opportunity for spontaneity in your love life. Even a pat on the bottom or a passionate kiss will keep your sexual intimacy alive.

begin to doubt whether your partner would really find you to be the beautiful heroine, if you shared this fantasy with him or whether he would think that the heroine should be thinner than you or more sexy? You can beat yourself up with self-doubt, until the idea of sharing this fantasy with him becomes terrifying. Why would you ever put yourself in a situation, where you may not match up in reality to your fantasy character? This explains in simple terms, why we so often keep our fantasies to ourselves.

 Lovers tip

Send each other text messages that remind you of your fantasy. You could say something like, 'The nurse would like to see you for your weekly check-up tonight.' This allows you the choice to step into character if it suits you. Put it in your diary, just by chance that you need a reminder.

A word of warning though: sometimes doing a role-play together can bring up your unconscious emotions. Don't underestimate how brave you both are for doing this. It shows that you have a great deal of commitment to feed your sexual intimacy together but it may be a roller-coaster ride at times. Let's face it, so is co-parenting as lovers. The way to success is through good communication.

On the other hand you may choose to get more adventurous and transform your fantasy into a role-play. First, you'll need a plot and what you want to do together when you get into role. Decide who you are and develop your character by finding the most appropriate clothes, wigs and props. The more you can create a visual impact with your character, the more you'll both feel like different people. No more Mum and Dad for the evening. It will help if you can get away from the reality of your domestic life. For some couples this may mean organising a babysitter and spending the evening in a hotel around the corner. There's no doubt that when you get away from home that the disturbances of babies, children, phones and email dissolve and you are able to let your hair down. Remember to go back to being Mum and Dad before you return home or this will be a sharp shock for your babysitter!

If you feel him struggling to accept you as a sexy lover now that you are a mother, take a bullish approach to help him to see the funny side of what he's thinking. Play the role of a prostitute and demand that he pays you for sex. Try to be as unemotional and businesslike as you can. You could also suggest a domestic exchange for your services; for example, he could pay for a blowjob by unloading the dishwasher or folding the washing.

A major threshold to cross as parents, is having your first night away together in a hotel. This is something that you would have taken for granted before you had children, but now it could seem almost impossible with a baby in tow. You'll need military-style organisation and planning to get this together. Think about your strategies well in advance and prepare for the unexpected. Another essential is childcare and back-up childcare just in case the first person has to cancel. They'll each need full training and briefing sheets about the day- and night-time routine and emergency contact numbers. That's a lot of administration.

♂ **His tip**

Have you ever spotted resistance in your system to engaging in these sexy, risqué scenarios with your partner? Or have you ever looked at her and thought that you couldn't possibly do that. Especially now that she's the mother of your child? Don't panic if you have. Try to observe your feelings and talk about them with her. She will be able to feel your ambivalence and you will reassure her if you are able to articulate how you are feeling. If you have intense feelings of disgust when you think of her sexually, then enlist the help of a therapist. (See the resources.)

I want to warn you gently that this first night away doesn't always live up to your expectations. How can it, with all the effort that it takes to get you there? Try not to set your hopes too high as it can sometimes take two or three attempts at going away together before you really feel the benefit. I have heard so many funny stories and not so funny ones about this first night away or attempt at it. You wouldn't believe how many children get sick the day before or how many parents get sick on rich food and alcohol at the hotel. The best story that I've heard was of the couple who were so tired by their life and the mammoth job of extricating themselves from their children that they drove down the road, parked up in a car park and fell asleep.

Try to be as relaxed as you can throughout this preparation phase. Remember that stress steals your energy and beauty. You're much better company calm than you are burnt out, in fancy underwear.

Never feel guilty about leaving your baby for the odd night, so long as your childcare arrangements are top-notch. Remember that you're leaving them behind so you can spend time with their father and this is a worthwhile investment for their future. They deserve to have parents who want to stay out and party together. Leaving behind your domestic responsibilities for 24 hours and regaining control of your life is part of the turn on. As are the luxury bath products, room service and fresh Egyptian cotton linen. There are a wonderful selection of couple-friendly, sexy hotels to suit all tastes and budgets, just do a quick search on the internet or a flick through the resources section to see what's out there. Some have exotic-themed bedrooms that may enhance your fantasies.

Month Six

Spending time away together isn't just about having really great sex. That's a bonus and to be truthful, it doesn't always happen the way you plan. So lower your expectations of swinging from the chandeliers for this trip. The greatest value of this one-on-one time is that you have a clear space to talk to each other. Couples tell me that they spoke more to each other on their first night away than they had in the previous six months. Try to choose a venue that has beautiful grounds and plenty of hidden corners to lounge around, should it pour with rain. Pack a sexy board game like Monogamy, not Monopoly, as a bad weather contingency plan. Not all couples get time away alone. This may be because the idea of leaving your baby behind is totally unacceptable. It's important that you listen to your own values and never feel pressured to do something that you're not comfortable with, even if you and your partner disagree. I also learnt a rule of parenting early on in my own career as a mum to never judge other parents if their way is different to mine. However, where there's a will, there's a way and you can still manage to steal precious moments together even with your baby in tow. Our world is at last compensating for the fact that the extended family has officially broken down so holiday establishments are now offering childcare facilities included in the accommodation. There are even luxury hotels with crèche and babysitting services and campsites with kids clubs.

♀♂ **Couple tip**

Begin to plan weekends away over the next year where you have the opportunity to do some activity together. It's fun to share hobbies and interests, even if you only get to do this once a year together. It's the intention that counts. You could do a cookery course, walking holiday or tantric sex course (see the resources). If you share the attraction, then go for it together. These are great birthday presents to buy for each other.

Going away with other mums and their babies doesn't always work out smoothly. It can be total chaos juggling all your different routines and sleeping patterns. It can be much more successful to go away for the weekend with your female friends or close female relatives, leaving your children at home with Dad for some quality bonding. It's always such a pleasure

Month Six

♀♂ **Couple tip**

If you prefer to self-cater then I strongly recommend that you take someone along to help you with the cooking and babysitting, or this could turn out to be no holiday for you. There must be a reason why so many couples split up when they return from holiday and I imagine that self-catering without help could be one of them. Consider also going on holiday with other parents where you can divide up the chores and ensure that you all get free time. Or find somewhere that includes help as part of the package.

when I see a new mum's eyes light up with excitement when she discusses her plans to go off for a girl's weekend after the baby has been weaned. It's something to look forward to through the early months. Most of the time as mums we are desperate to be pampered, so a health farm or a yoga retreat would be an obvious choice. If you live in the city, try to take a break in the countryside and if you live in the country, then I recommend that you stay there too. Plan your time away to give you maximum respite, pleasure and reconnection to yourself with a minimum of effort. Resist creating long tiring journeys or time changes for your body to have to adapt to.

The New Mum's Guide to Sex

I have always found incredible replenishment from spending time alone outdoors in nature. I like sharing my personal experience of this with other mums, because we can often be moving so fast through life with our baby on our hip and mobile to our ear, loaded with shopping bags, that we forget to stop and smell the roses. I will always carry the responsibility of motherhood with me, but this time that I spend out in nature is purely 'me' time, devoid of any responsibility other than to open myself up to the experience and be here now. It's about my sensual, intimate connection with the trees, the wind, the plants, the birds and even the mud and it goes something like this:

As I walk through a wood or across fields, I literally feel myself slow down, and the stress of my everyday life drop away. The weather excites my skin and wakes me up to the realisation that I am connected to all things. My feet sink in and out of the mud as I playfully allow myself to slip and slide around, just like the birds that weave in and out of each other or the squirrels that chase each other's tails. I invite you to join me here as I soften my pace alongside a majestic tree. I feel its strength and power as I lean back against its wise and gnarled trunk. Up above through its leaves, I can see the bright blue sky and the sunshine creating a dappled effect across my body. I begin an internal dialogue with myself here, it's a way for me to find out how I am doing in my life, especially how well I'm taking care and loving myself. I review my role as a mother, partner and

Month Six

friend. Sometimes, I gain enormous clarity in my head; other times my mind is as silent as the place where I am. I'm learning to accept that whatever happens here is the way it should be. The sheer beauty of the place humbles me and it touches my heart and connects me to my power as a sexual woman. I have a place here just as much as the animals, the plants and the trees, but I always remember to return home to my family, ready to re-engage with the reality of my everyday life. I hope that you will also find your place of nourishment wherever that may be.

8

Seven Months
and Beyond

If I were a magician, I'd wave my magic wand to help your ears and your heart to open wide to the message of this final chapter, which is this: do not be lazy in your relationship with your partner. Never take each other for granted or expect that you will be able to pick up where you left off years later, without working at your relationship. And always try your best to put your personal needs and desires before those of others. Never underestimate the reason why you are told to put your oxygen mask on, before you help others with theirs.

It's not the easiest of roads to travel, this rocky road of the early months and years of parenting together. It takes strength, courage and determination to become bigger and brighter people than you were before you began this journey. I know this to be true from my own personal experience, as well as what I've seen working with couples.

I hope that your hard work and commitment to your relationship over the past months will be beginning to pay off. But remember, that you can only do the best you can do, given your own personal circumstances. It always takes two to tango and sometimes things don't work out the way we intended or hoped that they would. With all the best will in the world, there are relationships that just can't make the transition into life as parents and it's important that we don't beat ourselves up over this. I'm not saying that you're not responsible for your actions, far from it, but I am asking you to be gentle and compassionate with yourself and each other.

RELATIONSHIP PROBLEMS

Any relationship break-up is incredibly painful. You have physically created another life through your love and if you decide to split up, you may fear that you're shattering this creation. There is no simple solution to separation but what matters most is the welfare of the children. I would advise you to get mediation to support you both to become excellent co-parents and friends, if only for the sake of the children. Couple counselling can be helpful to any relationship that is going through tough times. It really pays sometimes to take your struggle out of the home and to discuss it with a third party. See the resources for more details.

> ♀♂ **Couple tip**
>
> If you don't feel that you are ready to look for help outside your relationship, then I encourage you to keep looking for resolution between yourselves. One way is to use a talking stick whenever you're speaking about emotional issues. This idea comes from the Native American tradition and involves a stick or an object. The rule is that whenever you are holding the stick, you are the only person talking. Your partner listens to what you are saying and when you are finished speaking, you pass the stick on. Your partner then summarises what you've just said and you either agree or say it again. When you are happy that your point has been heard, your partner begins his/her talking time.

DOMESTIC VIOLENCE

It's important to mention that should either of you feel afraid for your personal safety, then this method would not be recommended. Sometimes it's hard to acknowledge difficult and dangerous patterns of behaviour when you are in them. To be clear, if you are being harmed physically in any way by your partner; hit, kicked, slapped or pinched or emotionally abused or controlled, then please talk to your GP about this right away. They will have the resources to make you and your children safe. You may be surprised how often this is happening to women (and occasionally men) in our society. If you recognise that this is happening to someone you know, please do not turn a blind eye but try to discuss it with them. It will be a relief for them to be able to talk to someone, as most victims of domestic violence keep quiet and feel guilty. This guilt is not surprising, as it may coincide with a time when you may be feeling low about your appearance or lack of libido. Try to recognise that although this post-natal time weakens your resolve, these incidents of violence could reoccur. Each time an act of violence is committed, the chances of it reoccurring become greater, with less time between incidents.

Every mother could benefit from doing a self-defence course that includes hands-on tactics to defend yourself against street, domestic and sexual attacks. You will gain confidence in your physical interaction with all people. This will show in how you hold yourself with power and self-authority and you will quickly learn to command and protect your own space.

♀♂ **Couple tip**
Attend a martial arts class together. You will learn good fighting techniques and increase your physical stamina. It's great fun to learn and flounder along together as beginners and as you both improve, it will be a turn-on to see your partner moving with trained and focused energy.

SINGLE MUMS

I'm happy to say that I've met many single mums with beautiful babies over the years and I take my hat off to you all. Some of you have chosen to have a baby without a partner. Whilst others have found yourselves faced with a relationship break-up early on into motherhood, for a variety of reasons. It's not easy to be alone at home with a small baby, especially through the long nights of feeding. I hope with all my heart that you have lots of loving and practical support from your family and friends through this time. Be kind to yourself. Start by lowering your expectations of what you can achieve on a daily basis and never beat yourself up for your situation. Every day holds the potential for new adventure. I know that this may seem like a wishy washy thing to say, but I truly mean it, so please believe me.

As the months pass, you may be open to the possibility of a new relationship. Remember that for every single mother, there will be an eligible single dad out there. It may be that you find a new Mr Right in cyberspace from your very own sofa.

Let's not fool ourselves into believing that we women are always the innocent victims in any relationship struggle or split because this just wouldn't be true, would it? We can give as good as we get, especially once we've regained our strength and equilibrium following childbirth. In many ways we can be just as aggressive as our men, only we do it in silent ways. Withdrawing sexual favours is a classic way we communicate our upset and resentment to our partners. Ouch. If you recognise that this is what you do, then you're more than halfway to stopping it. It's us mums who will lose out in the long run. Most men find it easier to open up emotionally after they have engaged sexually and as that is predominantly what we want from our relationships, we are shooting ourselves in the foot if we deny them this.

AFFAIRS

People have affairs and secret one-night stands when they feel that their relationship is lacking either emotionally or sexually. I'm sure you knew that already. What you may not know is what they gain from doing this, once the truth

> ♂ **His tip**
> Guys, I'm sorry to be so simplistic about your
> sexuality. I know that many of you come from
> your hearts when you communicate with your
> partners and good on you. But sometimes, it's
> better to call a spade a spade and be honest that
> sex will be one of the first things that comes to
> mind when you look at your woman.

is out and whether the affair fed their relationship in the long run. A lot depends on whether the other partner can regain his or her trust in the relationship.

I asked one mother, who had completely lost her libido following the birth of her second child, what had been the catalyst for her to reconnect to her sexuality (which she most certainly did). Her reply was that I wouldn't want to tell her story in this book, because she had had an affair and that was what had relit her fire and subsequently split up her relationship. I disagree with her, as I believe that we do need to hear this story because it serves as a wake-up call.

Think about how often you have heard of marriages, where one or both partners have long-term affairs and where the marriage survives in the knowledge of this. I know this happens for some couples along their parenting journey together.

There is no right way of doing relationships that suits all. What counts is being honest with each other about what is actually happening. Try to admit that there are bonuses for both partners in this set-up and that neither are the victims of a deception.

♀♂ Couple time

Wouldn't it be fantastic if you could get this magic ingredient, to feed your relationship without having to have an affair? Talk to each other about why you might consider having an affair and what the characteristics of your 'perfect' lover would be. Rise to the challenge and don't believe each other if you deny that the thought has never crossed your minds. Then challenge yourselves to design a fantasy role-play in which you play out your affair together. Better to stay faithful in reality and cheat in fantasy.

I'm not recommending that having an affair is a good way but it is an example of how we all have different ideas about what and how we want to be together. Sometimes during the course of a long-term relationship, our needs may change. There may be a time during your journey together when you might be happy that your partner is getting his sexual needs met in someone else's bedroom but that he still comes to you for friendship and emotional intimacy. We must never underestimate the great mystery of life. You can never be sure of the future as you read this today but you can be sure that you are clear about what is written (or spoken) in the agreement you have with your partner. Are you monogamous together, or are you non-sexual together or do you have an open relationship? These are big questions, but you do need to know the answer or else you may always fear the worst in the back of your mind. The existence of a contract is important as it gives your relationship a public face.

LOVE AGREEMENT

You may think that it is taking an extreme view to have an agreement between you and your partner but when you think about the complexities of your relationship as parents, lovers and friends, it's a sensible thing to do. I think we can sometimes take it for granted that we will be able to juggle the changes and challenges of life and that our relationships will be there to support this. Yes, it's true that a strong, loving relationship is your rock in rough seas but you both need to know what you expect. The simplest way to know the answer to this is to have regular and honest communication between you both.

It's too easy to bury your head in the sand in long-term relationships and to hide behind your children's hobbies and schedules. Years can go by before you stop and notice that your relationship isn't the one that you thought it was for all these years. You can be swept along by romantic love stories that you read about in magazines, but I challenge you to think today, what exactly you want from your relationship, especially in the context of being parents together. Then tell him.

> ♂ **His tip**
> I know that most of you would like life to be more straightforward, so wouldn't having a agreement with your partner help meet your needs? You could be clear about what is required of you in the role of father, lover and partner. Think about what you'd like in your relationship too.

So your relationship dream is what you would both like to do together in your relationship. This could be your shared dream to move to New Zealand or sharing the redesign of your garden at home as a place of sensual tranquillity with a football pitch or playground for your children.

You don't have to share your relationship dream with anybody — friends, family and, especially, your children. It's your private property.

♀♂ **Couple tip**

One new mother described to me how she and her partner would spend evenings together cutting out pictures from magazines and mounting them on cardboard. They were dreaming together of what they wanted in their relationship and displaying it in this visual, creative way. This is a wonderful way to transform your dreams of single life to family life. Remember to include pictures of your sexual dreams too.

♀♂ **Couple time**

So what could you include in your agreement? Here are a few suggestions:

• What kind of relationship do you want, is it monogamous (just having a sexual relationship with each other) or open or just parents without sex?

- How much time would you like to spend with each other alone (on a date) every week? Every month? Every year? This would include nights away together.

- How much time would you like to spend as a family (that's all of you together) doing an activity every week? Every month? Every year? This would include discussion about holidays.

- How much time would you like to spend alone or with your friends? This would include time away without your family.

- What are the relationship dreams that you share? (There is more about this later in the chapter.)

When you've thought, perused, discussed and hopefully agreed or agreed to disagree, then you will be ready to write up your agreement. Remember both to sign it. (Preferably, not with your blood.) You could redo this exercise every season if you wish or at least once a year.

HAVING MORE CHILDREN

There may come a time when you realise that your dream is expanding to include having another baby. This usually creeps up on women, on average about 18 months after giving birth. The maternal instinct is one of the most powerful energies known to man and once switched on, is a force not to be reckoned with. I want to encourage you to share your dream to have another child with each other as soon as possible. I say this because I know how easy it can be to conceive a second, third or fourth child. I must have heard the story of surprise at 'only doing it once and falling pregnant,' at least 500 times over the years. It still makes me smile. Yes, spontaneous sex on the stairs or a quickie before breakfast is fantastic but be aware that the fertility monster may be chasing you.

It's worth remembering, that unplanned pregnancies put an enormous pressure on your relationship. It's an emotional, environmental and financial stress to your stability. Sometimes the shock can be devastating, which is so sad, when it involves the miracle of a new life. Please drop the guilt if I'm describing you. Believe me, it is quite normal to feel like you've been hit by a bombshell if you conceive by surprise. Sometimes it can take the whole pregnancy to recover from the shock, other times it takes years and sometimes you never do recover. This is especially true for dads but it also happens to mums too.

♀♂ **Couple time**

If you are shocked speechless by an unplanned pregnancy then talk about it as much as possible. Talk to each other, to other parents and to your GP. It's not something to be ashamed of. It's a totally legitimate place to be, but if you suppress it then your resentment and anger will fester. Keep the channels of communication open between you both and have as much intimate physical time together as you can. (Look back at the earlier chapters for suggestions.) Only make your decision to try for a new addition to your family after having open and honest communication together. Playing tricks on each other will eventually come back and bite you in the bottom. If one of you really doesn't want to have another baby, now or never, then this point of view needs to be respected and discussed.

From the moment the thought of another baby pops into your head, be vigilant about your contraception. Pay attention to the extra-strong urge you get to rip his clothes off mid-cycle, as this will be the lovemaking session that makes you a family of four or five. If you have already had the conversation, then go for it and enjoy the potential double bonus of your sex together. By the way, when you're really turned on and orgasm, your chances of conceiving are better. Your cervix will dip into the ejaculate in your vagina as you orgasm and draw it into the uterus, increasing your potential for conception.

The longer the gap after your last baby, the better prepared your body will be for another pregnancy. Ideally you need to replenish your vitamins and minerals so that you are in optimum health before you try to conceive. Both of youshould address your diet and lifestyle habits for your best possible health. (See books that can advise you about this in the resources.)

♂ His tip

With all due respect, I know that it can be hard not to follow through when you're caught up in the throes of passion. Yes, you're unlikely to be able to stop and consider where she is in her cycle, but you will know if you are practising safe sex. If you haven't made up your mind whether you want another baby or not, then never, ever have sex without contraception. Not even a quick in and out, as there is sperm in your pre-ejaculate and she really could get pregnant from just this.

Another advantage of taking your time to conceive will be that you have more opportunity to really enjoy being lover-parents together. It's a shame if you are just getting your sexual intimacy back on track, after working hard at it and then you fall pregnant again. There's a risk that you won't be able to enjoy the beautiful garden of pleasure that you have created, as much as you might. Or at least for another year …

Be honest with yourself, is your only motivation to have sex with him to get pregnant again? Well, you wouldn't be on your own with this one. If this is you, try to reread the earlier chapters and see if this can change your motivation and whet your appetite a little. What I'm saying is, have sex because you really want to engage with your partner, because you fancy him and doing it. Goal-orientated sex just isn't rewarding for either of you and you can tell the difference.

FERTILITY AND CREATIVITY

Remember that even when you are sure that you don't want any more children, that you will still be fertile. If your contraception choices are secure then there'll be a minimal risk of pregnancy. This gives you a wide-open space to be fertile with your ideas and creations. When we no longer give birth to babies as women, we can give birth to our creative projects, like writing a book or painting a picture.

There'll be a period of gestation for all your creations and finally you will birth them into the world. Try your hand at different projects like creative writing, cooking, painting, clay work, etc until you find the one that speaks to you the most. This is an ideal way to spend your 'time out' from family life. It can be very sexually arousing to be creative. It seems that the more you create, the more juicy you get. The proof is in the pudding.

Gradually over the years, I have tried to train my children to give me space whenever I do my creative projects. Sometimes it works and sometimes it doesn't, it depends on their internal weather. What counts, is that they understand that I'm not rejecting them, but that I'm simply feeding myself first. They will always get their piece of my pie a little later and I'm much more able to give out to them unconditionally when I'm feeling full. They want to have this space for themselves too and we need to learn to respect this as their parents. Rest assured that, as the years go by and your children grow, that you will enjoy sharing creative projects with them, from play dough to sculpting together. Being able to relax with our children is one of the greatest gifts of being a mother. I know how difficult it can be to find the space and time to do this, as we all have such busy lives these days. We can also feel incredibly guilty if this doesn't work out or if we have a screaming match with them rather than the tennis match we planned. These feelings of guilt don't make us feel good;

they eat away at us and that's definitely not sexy. Aim to be an impeccable mum who tries her best and sometimes makes mistakes, but accepts that life isn't perfect. Now, this feels much more sexy, don't you agree?

Engaging with the overall design of how we run our family life is a very important project for us. So is the balance within our family, like which one of you tends to grab all the attention, particularly from you. In an ideal world everyone would get equal attention including you but in reality, family life is never this way. There will always be one of you having a crisis or who shouts and screams louder than the other and of course, this will be where your energy goes. What's important is that you don't hide behind these demands and use them as an excuse not to give yourself or your relationship quality time. Too much on-demand mothering needs to be banished, after the early months, so you can nourish your libido. I know this is harsh but that's the truth for you. I see this scenario too often in action and it can be our downfall as mothers. Children need to see that their parents are sticking together and celebrating their togetherness, rather than ducking and diving around each other and using the children as an excuse not to be intimate with each other.

It's good for our children to realise from a young age that mummy and daddy have private times together just as much as they have family times. This doesn't mean that you don't love your children as much as your partner; it's just a different sort of love. Over time, you will be gently introducing them to your family's way of life, or rather, to your family rules. This may be to not burst into your bedroom uninvited. If you have a lovely bouncy baby in your arms as you're reading this, then you may think that this can wait until later. As parents, these are our famous last words and this is how we get caught out by our own relaxed approach (or laziness). Remember that it won't be long before your bouncy baby becomes a thundering toddler and propels himself through your bedroom door, just as you and daddy are getting intimate together. None of us want to imagine this scenario, but it happens. Ask your friends who have older children — I'm sure they'll have a story to share.

I want you to be prepared for the next phase before it arrives. Many parents find it even more challenging and tiring to deal with the constant physical demands of a toddler. So, by giving yourself lots of opportunity for spontaneity and variety in where and when you have sex, will naturally increase your potential to get it together. By putting locks high up on doors around the house, you are stating your intent to the world to have sexual intimacy in your relationship. Even if you're struggling to find the time to be together, allow yourself to think about what you could get up to together behind a locked door and let this thought permeate into your mind as you prepare the dinner.

○♂ **Couple tip**

Put a lock on your bedroom door as soon as you read this. You may never need to use it if you train your children to knock. It's belt and braces. If you have a utility room, put a lock on the door, as you have lots of white noise in there. You may have an opportunity to have spontaneous sex on the washing machine one day and be so glad of the lock!

Every parent wants the best for their children; we want them to grow up to be well-balanced individuals. In their early life, we do our best to ensure that they are in nurturing and nourishing environments by choosing where they spend their day. When they're old enough to go out into the world on their own, we hope that we've given them enough training to keep them safe. Part of this training is about how to behave in a sexually intimate relationship and this will come directly from how we are in our relationship as parents. We provide our children with their main images of how two people have a sexual relationship and this is a big responsibility. Nobody does it perfectly and our children wouldn't want us to either. Despite this, we still have our fair share of guilt about not doing this job well enough and do you know what? I think we may sometimes have reason to feel this way. I wouldn't recommend feeling guilty about it though, as this will make you more tired than you are already. What counts is to recognise when you could have done better and make an intention to change something. This could be that you have the realisation that you've been letting your physical and emotional intimacy with your partner slip and that you're behaving more like siblings than lovers. It's unlikely that your baby will notice this but older children do notice how you are together, if only subconsciously. A good parental sex life is important for a strong family.

If you're finding this to be a difficult subject to discuss with your partner, then try to choose a time when you're in a good intimate phase together. It's much easier for him to listen to you, when you're pointing out how well you're doing together, rather than how you're not being successful as role models.

Healthy sexual role models do not hide their physical intimacy from their children but they do not flaunt it either. Kissing, hugging, holding hands and cuddling are all acceptable and healthy public images of intimate couples. Be proud to show the family, that Mum and Dad have physical contact and that you make space and time to be together privately. As the children grow, introduce family meetings as a forum to present your rules to protect your sexual relationship with a united front to the children. The younger they are, the simpler these will be. You will need to work out the rules yourself but one rule that we can all share, children and adults alike, is to knock and wait to be invited into each other's bedrooms. It's respectful this way. This is particularly important if you are leaving your mum persona at the bedroom door to find your sensual, sexual self, inside.

THE TRUTH ABOUT FAMILY LIFE

If we were truthful, most of us, given half the chance, would love to slip away and hide in a corner from the chaotic demands of family life. I have seen this silent, menacing game of battleships played out between couples, it even happens in my own home. How it goes is that we pretend not to be aware of each other but we are secretly watching their every move and waiting for them to make an escape bid. Either we intercept them and load them with chores or we watch them go and store up the resentment for later. Believe me that this is a very common scenario with all couples but especially those with babies and toddlers. It's human nature to want to have time off, without the constant physical and emotional demands of looking after children. Every parent has these feelings, no matter how much they wanted and tried for a baby.

♀♂ **Couple tip**

Step one is to recognise that this can be you on a bad day. Step two is to admit to each other how you can sometimes resent your job as a parent. Step three is to recognise when you are acting out your frustrations about your lack of freedom. You both need bucket loads of compassion for each other and a lot of trust that it is okay to tell your truth.

Sometimes our brains become befuddled after we have children and we seem unable to stop ourselves slipping into our old patterns of poor communication with each other. Let's not beat ourselves up over this but try to recognise how we could do it differently next time. Start saying how we're feeling, rather than waiting until it bursts out of you.

We all have our hopes and dreams of how we want to parent our children. Many of us have such high standards for this, fashioned on the trendy parenting styles of the day, that it can be a long way to fall if we don't fulfil these. I imagine that you've learnt this already, as some of these ideas don't match with how you behave at home. It's a matter of you finding your own natural way, but if this way is to behave like a domestic dictator, then you can expect a backlog of silent complaints from your partner for years to come. It's taken me more than a decade as a mum and therapist to realise this. I see now that all the unspoken resentment, disappointment and fears, can fester through the years and play havoc with our sex lives. It can literally shut us down sexually.

> ♂ **His tip**
>
> Many of you have told me that you can feel 'overwhelmed in an alien world' when you are with your family. Sometimes home can feel like a hostile environment ruled by a mum who has the full set of skills and aptitude for her job. You probably want to escape to the pub, to the gym, the golf course, to work or behind a newspaper. These feelings are normal, but be realistic and ask yourself: Do I 'put up and shut up' or stay around and express how I feel?

WHAT TYPE OF FAMILY ARE YOU?

Over the years, I have observed that most couples find themselves in one of four categories of domestic relationships. Whichever one you fall into will depend on a multitude of factors like your own childhood experience or your current financial situation. Of course, you can jump ship at any time. There's potential for resentment or harmony in each one but the depending factor, it seems, is how well you are able to communicate to each other.

'Modern' family

In this type of family unit, Mum and Dad juggle the demands of family life around their own careers. They try to assume an equal role in parenting.

Pros: Both parents get to have time to themselves pursuing their careers. There is a sense of balance in their roles and this creates a supportive and respectful atmosphere.

Cons: Both parents risk being exhausted by their demanding schedule and shared responsibility. Mum is more equipped by nature to juggle her work/life and this can create tension if Dad struggles to achieve this. Resentment could onset if they forget to share how they are feeling.

Sex life: They have a moderate to high potential for sexual connection based on how much they feel able to share their ups and downs.

Tip: Have a regular meeting together to discuss not just the practicalities of your week but also the emotional, mental and sexual aspects of it too. Through asking each other any questions or complaints about the schedule, their truth ball will start rolling.

'Traditional' family

Mum and Dad fulfil their individual roles. One or both of them goes out to work but once home, Dad makes it clear, albeit silently, that he's not too happy about having to do the never-ending list of chores.

Pros: Sometimes this situation suits Mum as it gives her a legitimate reason for her to not engage intimately with Dad because he is far too grumpy.

Cons: This silent and brooding resistance can be so uncomfortable that it pushes Dad out of the house to the golf club and the pub. Mum can then assume the role of the lonely victim in the relationship.

Sex: They have a moderate to low chance for sexual connection based on how often they spend quality time together. As such, Mum's desire for sex is probably low or at least with Dad it is.

Tip: Mum needs to insist that she has 'me' time every week to nourish herself. Design a weekly rota doing the chores between you both and try to laugh about how resistant you are towards them.

'Formal' family

Dad works long hours and Mum runs the home. Dad comes home from work most evenings in time to kiss the children goodnight and have dinner with Mum.

Pros: Both Mum and Dad have clear roles; Dad makes the

money and Mum runs the home. Mum may like it this way as she feels that dads just aren't capable of doing what she does. Dad gets to escape to work where it's less chaotic and he's in more control of his environment.

Cons: Dad could be so detached from family life that he can't relate to Mum and may even find her daily stories about the children a little boring. Mum could feel lonely.

Sex: Moderate potential for sexual connection especially if Dad shows how much he appreciates the good job Mum is doing with the children and Mum makes time to listen to Dad's work stories.

Tip: Mum needs good babysitters so she can either join Dad on work jaunts or have freedom to do her own thing. Dad should occasionally go in late or work at home to get an idea of the daytime routine.

'Adventure' family

Dad stays home and Mum goes to work. It could be that Dad is taking a career break or early retirement or simply that Mum earns more money.

Pros: Dad enjoys being with his children and learning new skills. Mum gets to fulfil her career and still be a mum. Mum is likely to feel more in charge of her life and consequently her libido.

Cons: Mum and Dad are beating at different paces and may miscommunicate. Mum may be far too tired once the children are in bed to contemplate anything other than sleeping. Dad has lots of opportunity to meet other mums who are happy to see him.

Sex: Moderate to high potential for sex if they are both feeling fulfilled by what they are doing and feeding their relationship with this sense of self-worth.

Tip: Dad needs to get out of the house regularly to do things with other men. Ideally Mum could organise to work from home one day a week to keep her connection with family life — working in her pyjamas would help with this.

Maybe you recognised your family in one of these descriptions or maybe you didn't. What I hope is that this has shown you that there is no one right or wrong style to parent together. There's certainly not a guaranteed method to keeping your sexual flame alive, although having good communication does go a long way towards this. Once you can communicate effectively about your feelings and emotions, you'll soon begin to express your sexual desires and dreams. Then the world will really be a more vibrant place with you in it.

It's never a good idea to have distance of any kind between you and your partner. I really don't believe the old saying that absence makes the heart grow fonder. I can think of many other ways to strengthen your heart connection,

> ## ♀♂ **Couple tip**
>
> Whenever you notice that your communication thread is ebbing or when you have a forced separation, I suggest the following tips to help you to keep connected:
>
> - Leave each other notes on the fridge or pillow about what you might like to do with each other when you next get the chance.
>
> - Send each other naughty text messages with sexual promises or reminders of your past sexual or romantic interludes.
>
> - Post a 'Lovers cheque' to your partner with a promise of a sexy engagement.
>
> - Email each other links to sexy sites.
>
> - Put a sexy dot-to-dot drawing in your partner's 'to do' pile.

effective communication being top of my list. And as we're so spoilt for choice with all the many ways to communicate globally, there's no reason not to be having regular intimacy, especially via webcam. Thankfully, we no longer have to rely on the ancient art of letter writing, although love letters are still pretty cool – hint, hint. But the choice to do this will always be yours. Let's face it, you can be in the same room as each other and sleep in the same bed night after night and still feel a physical distance between you.

Being in a long-term committed relationship that includes bringing up a family, will always present challenges and it's natural that we would want to distance ourselves from situations that are potentially painful and ugly. We can even distance ourselves from who we truly are and from our potential to be really juicy, sexy mums. Yes, I know this is still hard to swallow, but try to see this truth as a springboard to power. We all need to creatively build bridges across this distance if we are to keep up our intimacy and sexual connection with all things.

The A–Z
of how to
Rediscover your Passion

A is for arousal, acceptance, adventure, asking and action.

B is for body, breasts, beautiful, breathing, brain, brave and bathing.

C is for compassion, coupling, constructive, creative, contraception and cooperation.

D is for dancing, dressing up, drive, dream, determination, daring and developing.

E is for easy, enjoy, energy, erotic, entertainment, escaping, ecstasy and email.

F is for fantasy, frivolity, fun, forgiveness, forgetting, future, flowers and freedom.

G is for goals, glamour, gorgeous, gentle, generous, great, guilt and genuine.

H is for harmony, horny, hilarity, happiness, health, hope, healing and holidays.

I is for intimacy, intention, imagination, ideas, involvement and interest.

J is for juggling, joking, juicy, jealousy, joy and jobs.

K is for kissing, kinky, kindness, kit, keepsake, kitchen and knickers.

L is for libido, love, lust, laughter, like, longing, life, luxurious and lactation.

M is for mind, masturbation, masculine, model and more.

N is for notes, normal, nurture, negotiate, network, near, navigate and naughty.

O is for orgasm, observation, organise, options and opportunity.

P is for pleasure, positive, play, process, perseverance and please.

Q is for question, queen, quality and quote.

R is for receptivity, role-play, reality, recognition, relationship and remembering.

S is for sex, share, seduction, suck, senses, sensual, sublime, savour and saucy.

T is for toys, trust, touching, tactile, try, throb, think, tickle and tip.

U is for upward, unique, urge, uniform, upstairs and underwear.

V is for verbal, view, vagina, vision, victory, variety, value, Venus and vivacious.

W is for want, wish, wobble, water, wild and woman.

X is for X-rated.

Y is for yummy, yes, yoga, yippee, youth and yesterday.

Z is for zip, zing, zest and Zen.

MORE WORDS OF ENCOURAGEMENT

I wanted to thank you for taking the time to look through this book. I hope that it has given you ideas and inspired you to become the sexy mum that you are and always have been. Most of us just need a gentle reminder after we have a baby and it has been my great pleasure to give this to you. Being sexy isn't about being able to swing from the chandeliers, although that could be a good dinner-party trick. It's about listening to your desires and allowing them to flow through you into your everyday life. No matter how dull, mundane and stressful life may seem at times. Touching yourself and all others with softness, sensuality and beauty will get you further along the road to maternal fulfilment than a quick cappuccino and a muffin with the girls. Although, I do believe that a little of what you fancy lights your fire too. We are, after all, human beings and all of our hungers need to be fed.

Sexual desire is one of our best human qualities and like all things, it will ebb and flow throughout your life. It's natural to have low times and high times, so remember to celebrate it when you have it and then be patient for the next wave to come. I'm hoping that you have created strategies for yourself to win back your lust and passion and that one of these will be rest and relaxation. Have you noticed by now that whenever you chill-out about firing up the passion, it seems to happen more easily? Tiredness is never good for your libido and nor is stress. So remember never to push yourself, especially in the early months. Sleep whenever you can and then wake up dancing. This is the best way to dance all your dreams and fantasies into reality.

If I could give you a final piece of advice about how to rediscover your passion after childbirth it would be this: keep everything in your life as simple as possible. Keep your social diary simple, your wardrobe simple, your diet simple, your hobbies simple and the children's life simple. In this way you will have stress-free space to truly explore who you are as a sexy mum. I wish you this simple way, as you truly deserve it.

Appendix

EXTERNAL GENITALIA

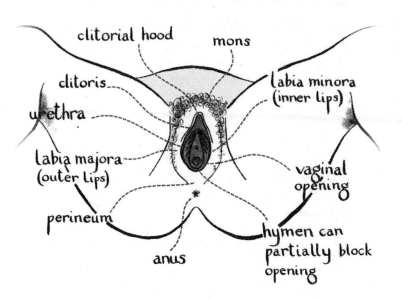

clitorial hood   mons

clitoris   labia minora (inner lips)

urethra

labia majora (outer lips)

vaginal opening

perineum

anus

hymen can partially block opening

VISUALISATION

If possible, please record yourself reading this. Try to be relaxed and calm as you make the transcript. Take your time, there's no rush.

I invite you to come with me now as we take a gentle stroll together in nature. Let me help you to discover your own space of stillness and inner peace. This place is always available to you right here and now, for you to access a state of deep rest and relaxation. Perhaps you already have an intimate knowledge of this special place – it exists deep inside you, it's your birthright as a human being and a necessity as a busy mum. It truly belongs to you, yet it is easy to forget that this possibility to relax and let go is just a breath away. So just for today, just for these precious moments, I ask you to put down your everyday tensions and rediscover yourself.

Begin by finding a comfortable place to lie down, where you know that you will be physically comfortable and undisturbed for at least half an hour. Give yourself permission to let your body sink into the softness underneath you, as you feel yourself relaxing and releasing tension, stress and strain from every part of your body. Let your inner eye guide you from the tip of your toes to the top of your head. Imagine that you're being carried along on a cloud and that your body is becoming weightless as your mind becomes more and more empty of thoughts. Dream of floating on this soft and fluffy cloud; you have nothing to do, not a care in the world. All you need to do is enjoy these sensations flowing through your body.

I invite you now to take three deep breaths into the lowest part of your stomach. As you take each breath in through your nose feel it travelling all the way deep into your pelvis, expanding and softening the space down there, and as you exhale feel yourself releasing any pain, tension or tightness. I encourage you to tune into your pelvis and genital area and to acknowledge any numbness or pain you may be experiencing down there. Maybe you're unaware that you've been holding this inside your body since your pregnancy and birth, it's quite natural for this to happen. So set your intention now to consciously release this as you breathe out slowly through your mouth. Visualise yourself blowing three long, slow breaths down a straw.

Use your breath to connect with your body. As you breathe in through your nose imagine that a beam of white light is softly filtering into the top of your head and running the length of your spine, down your legs and finally into the ground. In the same way, as you breathe out see this beam of light changing colour as it travels back up through your body and out your head. Let your breath be soft and slow, so that you become aware of every hair on the inside of your nostrils blowing in the breeze of your inhalation.

Allow your breathing to return to normal and simply observe how naturally it snakes in and out of your body.

Acknowledge that you don't need to do anything, as breathing is a natural process that doesn't require any effort. Enjoy this sensation and compliment yourself on your ability to allow your body this momentary rest and relaxation. You know that you are not responsible for anyone now but yourself and this may feel like pure bliss. Relish this possibility. Even at times of tiredness, stress and physical exhaustion, your mind, body and spirit have always got the potential to access deep, restorative healing. Your powerful mind can influence and affect your body if you allow it to. Deep healing and cellular transformation is all within the realms of possibility, as you become more and more willing to step deeper and deeper into full body relaxation. As you engage with this change and transformation, notice how your breath becomes even softer.

Walk with me now on this magical journey of discovery to find a special, safe place. Maybe you can already see it in the distance but remind yourself that there is absolutely no hurry or stress to get there. You have all the time in the world and wherever you are right now is perfect for you. Come through the gate that leads you into a beautiful park, full of trees, grass and flowers. Notice how your body moves with a relaxed pace, as you make your way across the soft green grass, their blades tickling your toes and caressing the soles of your feet. Let these sensations awaken your whole body. Stand still for just the briefest of moments and take another deep breath in through your nose, this time connecting with the earth under your feet. Feel the power and fertility of the earth and imagine that you are breathing this natural force of strength inside you. As you breathe out, let go once more of any physical stress or strain and channel it back down into the earth.

Pay particular attention to your fantastic pelvis and acknowledge all the hard work and support it has provided by creating a container of love, warmth and nurturance for a new precious life. Feel into your womb space and recognise that it is transforming back into a healthy, vibrant, creative, fertile space, ready to receive new ideas or new life. I encourage you to search inside to find the flame that burns deep within this place of power. Keep looking and believing that you will see it, no matter how low it flickers. Trust that your flame of passion is still alive within you. This flame is your spark, your illumination and your imagination. It links you up with the all-powerful force of creativity, in particular the creative forces of nature. Trust that you have the capacity within you to fan your fire and see it burning ever bright within your belly. Know that like the phoenix, who rises from the flames reborn, you will travel through this transition from woman to mother.

Become aware of the golden sunlight caressing your body and notice how easily and naturally the heat from the inner fire that is rising within you meets and merges with the warmth from the sun. As you open your eyes, see the bright light illuminating the beautiful garden around you. The flowers, trees and insects are all basking in this glorious sunlight; watch how they become bigger, brighter and full of life as they reach up towards the sunlight. Notice how you too are beginning to stretch upwards in an attempt to take more of the sun's nourishment within you. Your skin rejoices from the touch of the rays and your spine lengthens and stretches out. Take three deep breaths once again, and imagine that as you breathe in through your nose, that you are breathing this golden sunlight down the length of your spine. With each breath notice how the spaces between your vertebrae increase in size and fill up with this light. Enjoy this sensation of freedom and lightness that you are creating for yourself along your spine. Give permission for any lingering muscular tensions to melt from you now.

Allow your attention to be drawn now to the magnificent flower garden and let yourself be magnetically pulled towards your favourite flower, just like a bee is drawn to the succulent nectar.

Admire the perfection of this flower, its pure beauty, its colour, its delicacy and its divine fragrance. Take a deep breath in through your nose, becoming aware of its aromatherapy. Let the sensations that this arouses in your body literally fill you up. Close your eyes for a moment to appreciate just how much the flower's vibrant, pure colour continues to stimulate your mind and sensations. Look at this flower as if you were looking through Alice's looking glass and see every finite detail of Mother Nature's grand design.

Realise that your anatomy is just as intricate in design as this flower, especially your private places, sometimes hidden behind folds of skin like the petals of this flower. Gently squeeze and release your pelvic floor muscles, softly, softly to draw your attention to your genital area. You will have intimate knowledge of this place, having given birth through there just a relatively short time ago. I encourage you now to look around you, to find a comfortable spot in this divine garden where you can lie down. Take your time, gently relaxing onto the earth; perhaps you can feel the soft grass moulding against your body or maybe you are shaded from the sunlight by the branches of a wise old tree. Enjoy this time of relaxation, here in this beautiful garden, all alone without a care in the world.

As you lie there in this safe and magical place, take your focus to your vagina, giving yourself permission to make a journey down there, at least with your mind. Notice how you feel, as I invite you to make friends with this place and to honour and thank it for being a beautiful birthing canal to your baby. Imagine that you are gently touching the outside lips of your vagina with the same delicate finger pressure that you would use to stroke the petals of your favourite flower. Feel that as you caress the outside of your vagina you are introducing love and healing to this area. Acknowledge any emotions that surface, as you hold this image of yourself lying in a fragrant flower garden, touching your vagina like the most delicate of flowers and let this positive visualisation heal you.

Notice how your relaxation encourages the entrance to your vagina to relax and soften. Imagine that you have tiny, sparkly lights shinning out of your fingertips and let these beam inside your vagina. See how the inside walls begin to sparkle like a crystal cave and you're able to see that your pc muscles are even stronger and more powerful than before you gave birth. Know that this light is a healing light and its purpose is to help repair and rejuvenate any physical or emotional scarring inside your genitals. Whether this be from the process of childbirth or from any trauma.

Open up and let go of old hurts and quickly replace them with new life. This is your opportunity to reawaken your sex centre, relight your fire and step into a new place of power and adventure as a sexy mum.

This potential is always here in your garden. All you have to do is to remember this time and know how to find your way back here.

Slowly, very slowly I invite you to open your eyes and to get up from the ground feeling refreshed, rejuvenated and inquisitive to know more of who you are. Walk with me now with light steps back across the garden, passing the divine flowers and back to your everyday life.

Resources

LATE PREGNANCY

A healthy diet for your pregnancy

I recommend you read *The Gentle Birth Method* by Dr Gowri Motha for information about what foods you should and shouldn't eat during your pregnancy. There are also recommendations for Ayurvedic herbs and supplements that will help to prepare your body for a gentle birth. It's a tried and tested method and I cannot recommend her work enough. Try Dr Motha's Ayurvedic food. You will also find instructions for the vaginal stretching in the gentle birth book and perineum massage oil.

For more information, visit: www.gentlebirthmethod.com

A shopping list for your birth and early post-natal months

I always encourage my clients to buy everything they will need for the birth and the early post-natal weeks in the last month of pregnancy. It's a lot – here is an outline of what I recommend:

For the birth you may need:

Essential oils: Clary sage, Jasmine, Frankincense.

Bush flowers: Clear and clam spray, this helps to chill you out through the birth.
You can buy these from the Nutri Centre website, www.nutricentre.com

Birthing harmony by Dame Diana Mossop: a set of flower essences to support you to have an easier birth. I would also recommend visiting her to recover from the birth for both the baby and the mother. www.phytob.com

Massage oil:
www.activebirthcentre.com

Homeopathic set, available from Helios Pharmacy at:
www.helios.co.uk

Have a present and card to give to Dad during the birth. Write him a message from your heart that will give him some support and give him a gift that will distract him. One mum gave her partner a wildlife photographic book, as this was his passion.

For the early post-natal months you may need:
Essential oils: Rose Otto essential oil, lavender essential oil, post-natal bath oil.
www.activebirthcentre.com

A herbal bath infusion of marjoram flowers, comfrey leaves, and St John's wort leaves and flowers will help heal your perineum. (You will need a handful of each herb in your bath.)
www.baldwins.co.uk

Holistic practitioners experienced in working with pregnancy
Viveka is an integrated health-care practice, headed up by consultant obstetrician, Yehudi Gordon. His team is dedicated to

working with mothers and babies. You can make appointments for nutritional advice, acupuncture, homeopathy, cranial sacral therapy, sex therapy, counselling, healers and much more.
www.viveka.co.uk

Sexy pictures taken of you both to remember your sexy pregnant shape
Have a beautiful painting of you at this special time.
www.dubowski-art.com.

Or why not have some photos taken?
www.tinabolton.com

Body shapes and body sculpture
Have your pregnant tummy and breasts cast for you to treasure forever.
www.jamiemccartney.com

Be creative in your pregnancy
Workshops and one-to-one sessions where pregnant women can paint, sculpt and chill out. Helping to prepare you for birth and early motherhood.
www.womantomother.co.uk

Want to learn how to masturbate?
www.bettydodson.com

www.householdcompanion.com

www.sense-and-sensuality.com

Courses to increase your sexual confidence and knowledge.
www.amoralondon.com

A DVD that can help – *Better Sex Video: Becoming Orgasmic DVD*, directed by Dr Mark Schoen PhD, Sinclair Institute, 1993

Find a doula
A doula will support you during the birth but may also be
available to help you out in the early post-natal weeks to give
you a chance to recover.
www.doula.org.uk

Have a romantic break together before the birth
www.mrandmrssmith.com

www.myhotels.com

MONTH ONE
Recover from bad birth memories, trauma and post-natal depression
It is always best to read about the therapist on their website, then
call up with your questions or have a preliminary meeting before
you commit to ongoing sessions.

See above for more details about the therapists at Viveka.
www.viveka.co.uk

To find a qualified counsellor in your area try:
www.relate.org.uk

MONTH TWO
Increase your lubrication
There are many excellent water-based lubricants on the market
but be sure that you read the label to be sure that they are
compatible with your form of contraception. You also need to be
sure that you want the sensations they promise such as tingling
or heat.

I would recommend the Durex range because you can buy them in the supermarket or order from www.durex.com and have them delivered to your door.

Sexy underwear for breastfeeding and playing
The top feeding bra amongst mums was the Elle Macpherson La Mere Maternity Bra.
www.figleaves.com.

Functional and also sexy is the post-natal waist-trimming girdle designed by Dr Gowri Motha in conjunction with Agent Provocateur. There are more feeding bras in the same range.
www.agentprovocateur.com

Anal stimulation for his pleasure
Look at the nexus excel. This gives him intense sexual pleasure by massaging the prostate gland.
www.sextoys.co.uk

Plenty of lubrication – maximus is the best for anal pleasures.

Sexy coupons
Forty-four coupons full of seductive suggestions to surprise your partner.
www.sextoys.co.uk

Month Three
Shape and style your bits 'down there'
www.smoothshave.co.uk

Sex toys for your PC muscles
The 'Cone' is an innovative hands-free sex toy and as you sit on

it you can squeeze your muscles around it. The Berman Center Juno Weighted Pelvic Exerciser should keep you practising.
www.sextoys.co.uk

The Kegelmaster — regular use is key to success with this pelvic floor toner.
www.kegelmastereurope.com

Smart Balls for training the PC muscles.
www.funfactory.de

Suspect that you have vaginismus, dyspareunia, erectile dysfunction or premature ejaculation?
Contact a sex therapist.
www.basrt.org
www.relate.org.uk

STD check up or other sexual health concern?
Contact Doctor Christian Jessen who specialises in sexual health issues.
www.samedaydoctor.co.uk

Month Four

Contraception
Have a look at the ovum cervical cap, you can buy it over the counter in Boots. It gives you up to 70 hours protection in one stretch. Have it fitted/checked by your GP.
www.oves.com

Honey cap
This cervical cap is stored in honey when not in use and doesn't require extra spermicide. It can also be left in you for up to 50 hours.
Call Shirley Bond on: 020 7935 0023.

Nutritional support to rebalance hormones
Contact Marilyn Glenville and her team consult at Viveka.
www.viveka.co.uk

Getting turned on
Some women like to watch DVDs, some enjoy reading erotic
literature or other women's fantasies while others get off from
listening to erotic stories. You will only know your thing by
trying and your taste may change from day to day.

Check out Anna Span's films, Britain's first female porn
director.
www.sextoys.co.uk

Experiment with erotic stories. Have them on your iPod and no
one will know.
www.earotica.co.uk
www.whispersmedia.com

MONTH FIVE
Websites to keep you connected with other mums
www.netmums.com
www.huggiesclub.com
www.mums-room.co.uk
www.babycentre.co.uk

Personal shopping to change your wardrobe
www.topshop.co.uk

Sexy, quality clothes for dressing up in, for that special night in
together.
info@weareallcourtesans.com

DVDs to learn to strip
www.mypole.co.uk

Burlesque dance classes
Learn to dance with professional burlesque dancers and meet
other mums who have transformed their self-confidence
through learning this dance.
www.ministryofburlesque.com
www.amoralondon.com

Take a nap with the Catnapper CD
Thirty minutes for deep restorative sleep. The ultimate power-
nap for mums.
www.hemi-sync.com

MONTH SIX
Massage for pleasure
I would recommend simple olive oil mixed with two drops of
ylang-ylang essential oil.
For special occasions try Durex Massage and lubricant. This is an
excellent product as it can multitask.
www.durex.com

Love Licks is a playful kit containing a bottle of warming oil,
body dust and gel.
www.sextoys.co.uk

Good clean love passion candle
The candle heats up the oil for a sensual warm massage.
www.amoralondon.com

Coconoil is a divine body cream that liquefies in your hands to make
an excellent massage oil. Add to it your favourite essential oil.
www.coconoil.co.uk

Resources

Your sexy house
Fill it with adventure from the many toys, DVDs, games and ideas that are available.
www.sextoys.co.uk

Include candy lingerie, Rub my Duckie, Incognito Mascara and lipstick vibe, vanilla bondage kit and dressing-up clothes.

Play the Monogamy board game together for those rainy days.
www.monogamyonline.com

Choose coffee table books and art prints to suit your erotic taste.
www.obsessionart.com

For a sexy course on your own or with your partner
www.tantralink.com
www.amoralondon.com
www.householdcompanion.com
www.sense-and-sensuality.com

Cookery course that will transform your eating habits and boost your energy.
www.montsebradford.com

Time away
I can personally recommend the following hotels and retreats. They have been a lifesaver in their own way over the years.

For a sexy night away with a twist or a theme.
www.myhotels.com
www.blanchhouse.co.uk
www.crazybeargroup.com

With the children in tow and still be able to relax.
www.babingtonhouse.co.uk
www.cowleymanor.com
www.ickworthhotel.com
www.luxuryfamilyhotels.com

For a really relaxing and rejuvenating time away.
www.middlepiccadilly.com

MONTH SEVEN

Cyberdating
www.date.com
www.passion.com
www.dating4parents.com

Couple counselling
www.relate.org.uk

Self-defence courses for women
Intensive courses available in UK.
www.wutan.no

Worried about your behaviour towards your partner?
www.respect.uk.net

References

Ballard, Collin (2005) *The Guild of Erotic Artists, Volume One*, The Guild of Erotic Artists, Hertfordshire

Berkmann, Marcus (2005) *Fatherhood: The Truth*, Random House, London

Burton, Richard and Anderton, Sophie (2003) *The Essential Kama Sutra*, Erotic Print Society, London

Burton, Sir Richard and Arbuthnot, F. F (2005) *The Pop-Up Kama Sutra*, Stewart, Tabori and Chang, New York

Cameron, Ian (2005) *Masterclass: Going Down*, Erotic Print Society, London

De Angelis, Barbara (1998) *Secrets About Men Every Woman Should Know*, Element, New York

Dickson, Anne (1985) *The Mirror Within: New Look at Sexuality*, Quartet Books, London

Eddison, Sadd (1995) *Really Naughty Dots*, Connections, Buckingham

Friday, Nancy (2003) *Men in Love*, Ransom House, London

Glenville, Marilyn (2001) *The Nutritional Health Handbook for Women*, Piatkus Books, London

Gordon, Dr Yehudi (2002) *Birth and Beyond*, Vermilion, London

Grace, Janey Lee (2005) *Imperfectly Natural Baby and Toddler*, Orion Publishing, London

Grace, Janey Lee (2005) *Imperfectly Natural Woman*, Crown House Publishing Ltd, New York

Hare, Jenny (2007) *Orgasms and How to Have Them: A Guide for Women*, Fusion Press, London

Hooper, Anne (2005) *Erotic Massage*, Dorling Kindersley, London

Heiman, Julia and LoPiccolo, Joseph (1988) *Becoming Orgasmic*, Simon and Schuster, New York

Kitzinger, Sheila (1985) *Woman's Experience of Sex*, Dorling Kindersley, London

Lalvani, Vimla (1999) *Yoga for Sex*, Hamlyn, London

Lightwoman, Leora (2003) *The Beginner's Guide to Tantric Sexuality DVD*, New World Music Ltd, London

Lindberg, Marrena (2001) *The Orgasmic Diet*, Piatkus, London

Lorius, Cassandra (2003) *Tantric Secrets*, HarperCollins, London

Martyn, Elizabeth (2001) *Baby Shock!*, Vermilion, London

Metcalfe, Alice (2003) *Masterclass: Blowjobs*, Erotic Print Society, London

Mitchell, Allison (2006) *Time Management for Manic Mums*, Hay House, California Motha, Dr Gowri and Macleod, Karen (2006) *Gentle First Year*, Harper Thorsons, London

Motha, Gowri and Swan Macleod, Karen (2004) *The Gentle Birth Method*, Harper Collins, London

Royalle, Candida (2006) *How To Tell A Naked Man What To Do*, Piatkus Books, London

References

Sampson, Val (2006) *The Real Sex Kitten's Handbook*, Quadrille Publishing, London

Scarlet magazine for women: www.ScarletMagazine.co.uk

Sharkey, Harriet (2006) *Pregnancy (Collins Need to Know?)*, Collins, London

Stubbs, Kenneth Ray and Saulinier, Kyle Spencer (2000) *Erotic Passions*, Penguin, London

Sundahl, Deborah (2004) *Female Ejaculation and the G-spot*, Fusion Press, London

Woodall, Trinny and Constantine, Susannah (2006) *Trinny & Susannah: The Survival Guide — A Woman's Secret Weapon to Getting Through the Year*, Weidenfeld & Nicolson, London

Zilbergeld, Bernie (1993) *The New Male Sexuality*, Bantam, New York

About the Author

Rachel Foux has undertaken many formal studies and professional qualifications over the past 15 years to support her client work including counselling, reflexology, spiritual healing and most recently a Relate psychosexual therapy training course. Rachel believes that her own personal experiences and diverse training enhance her depth of knowledge in the field of sexuality. In particular, her study of the teachings of tantra and spiritual sexuality greatly inspire her work.

Rachel has a special interest in working with couples and women through their child birthing years, helping them to share a positive experience of birth and to remember that they are lovers as well as parents. This has been the focus of her work for some years, both individually with clients and through presenting workshops.

Most recently, she is a resident sexpert at Amora, the academy of sex and relationships, which is based in London.